I'll Show Them Who's BOSS

THE SIX SECRETS OF SUCCESSFUL MANAGEMENT

GERRY ROBINSON

Published by BBC Books, BBC Worldwide Ltd,
Woodlands, 80 Wood Lane, London W12 0TT

First published 2004 by BBC Worldwide Ltd
ISBN 0 563 52139 2

Commissioning editor: Emma Shackleton
Project editor: Sarah Lavelle
Copy editor: Steve Dobell
Designer: Ann Thompson
Production controller: Christopher Tinker

Set in Quay
Printed and bound in Great Britain by The Bath Press

For more information about this and other BBC books,
please call 08700 777 001 or visit our website on www.bbcshop.co.uk

Contents

Acknowledgements

I would like to thank all of those who so generously and courageously invited me into their businesses and families, and who often revealed to me some of their innermost secrets. Without them it would have been difficult to show some of the obvious problems and opportunities in business.

I would also like to thank all of those at the BBC who have participated in making the programmes, in particular Michelle Kurland and Kelly Webb-Lamb, who got the thing off the ground.

Most of all, thanks to Jane Ross-Macdonald, without whom this book would simply not have been written.

Preface

In setting out to write this, I faced something of a dilemma. I have always been a staunch critic of books on management. I have, almost without exception, hated every management or business book that I have read, or – to be more honest – started to read. At the heart of this is a feeling I have that they always seem to complicate rather than to simplify the issues involved in running a business.

On the other hand I have always loved what might loosely be called guide-books. Whether it is a guide to how to get the best from a visit to the Sistine Chapel or how to build a tree house, I love them. There is a point to them. They don't philosophize about the rights and wrongs of building tree houses or explore the geometric formulae involved in their construction. They just tell you, as simply as possible, how to get on with it. Admirable.

That may all sound very simplistic and, if it does, good. I'm not pretending that the issues involved in running a business are always as straightforward as a visit to the Sistine Chapel or building a tree house, but the principle of seeking simplicity is equally applicable to both, and, to be honest, I do firmly believe that running a business is more simple than people generally imagine.

If you'd picked up a book on building tree houses (which incidentally might be the better choice!) then it would be a fair assumption that that's what you want to do. The fact is that you've picked up this one, so I assume you're interested in management. Put the tool kit down and follow me.

▶ The six secrets of successful management

Gerry has given us the confidence to see that we are capable, and just to get on and do it

The first series of *I'll Show Them Who's Boss* was broadcast by the BBC in 2003; the second series a year later. Each episode showed what happened when I was invited into a family business that needed help in some way. The key players opened up their financial affairs and their hearts in a way that amazed and touched me, and in each case I was able to pinpoint very early on where the roots of their troubles lay, as outsiders often can. Everyone was delighted, at first. What was then challenging – and potentially explosive – was the unfolding process of working out and communicating the often unpalatable solutions. I certainly set the cat among the pigeons! The companies needed new leaders, they needed to let people go, they needed to focus on goals, they needed to change with the times, and they needed to be better at communication. What was fascinating was that these very different businesses *were all making similar mistakes*.

Each episode lasted less than an hour, and yet each took months to make and resulted in many hours of film. I was conscious that there was much more I wanted to say that, because of the way television works, I couldn't. This book is the answer. In writing it I have drawn on a lot of material that did not appear in the films, and on my own business experience, to offer something more than the television programmes in themselves could do. Real, practical advice on the key things you need to get right in order to run a successful business. In the following chapters I will use the stories from both television series to illustrate what I call the Six Secrets of Successful Management.

1 Leadership

All successful companies have one leader who understands how to lead and knows what he or she is doing. I will show you what it means to be a leader and whether you have got what it takes.

2 Taking Charge of the Future of Your Business

You need to have a vision, and you must learn how to formulate a strategy for the future, communicate it with a passion, and ensure it gets carried out.

3 Getting Commitment from Your Work-force

People are the life-blood of your business, and you're lost if your people aren't all singing from your hymn sheet. This chapter is all about good people management – how to find them, how to manage them, and how to keep them happy.

4 Doing the Dirt – Once

Business leaders occasionally need to make tough decisions. Good leaders do it cleanly and kindly. Find out how to do this hardest of tasks properly, so that you can move the business forward with confidence.

5 Rising Above the Detail

Micromanagement is a common mistake, but it is a disastrous path to go down. Good managers need to focus on the big picture. I will show you what information you really need, and what you can do without.

6 Communication

This word is often bandied about by people who don't know what they're talking about. I don't mean spin, I mean honest-to-goodness telling it how it is in a way that can't be misunderstood. I also mean getting your passion and vision for the company across to colleagues in a meaningful and inspiring way.

I have added two further chapters. One is about family dynamics and how they affect businesses. This is not only because *I'll Show Them Who's Boss* focused on family firms, but also because so many businesses in the UK are actually family-run. Add to this all those businesses that are started by friends, and you've got thousands of complex relationships causing problems in meeting-rooms across the country. I think it's a really interesting area, and I've highlighted several ways in which you can avoid the most common pitfalls. The last chapter seeks to debunk various management myths. I have sometimes been criticized for my somewhat unorthodox style, but, hell – it's worked for me, and I want to correct some common misconceptions that most people accept as gospel truth. If you only read one chapter in this book, read this one!

Let me introduce you to the eight companies that I'll be referring to throughout this book to illustrate the management points I will be making.

● AMT Espresso, London

Set up ten years ago, this chain of coffee bars was run by the half-English, half-Mexican McCallum-Toppin brothers. It had grown quickly and, at the point I arrived, had 37 kiosks in airports and railway stations around the UK with a staff of 350 and a turnover of £11 million. Originally the three brothers had been encouraged by their father, but since his death a year previously continual bickering and lack of co-operation between them had begun to hinder their growth plans. Although they had split some management tasks up (youngest brother Alastair dealt with company development; middle brother Allan dealt with staff; oldest brother Angus was the buyer), I could see immediately that it was vital for one of them to provide clear leadership if the company was to continue to thrive in an increasingly competitive industry.

● George Brown & Sons, Wiltshire

This was a long-established fruit and vegetable wholesaler run by a co-operative of eighteen family members. For over a century things had pottered along fairly smoothly, but in the last fifteen years the market had changed dramatically with new competition from supermarkets and, although turnover was £1.4 million, profits were nose-diving. The owners were the brothers Paul and David Brown, and their cousin Jim, all in their fifties. Coming up behind them were Paul's children Lorraine, Ruth and Phillip, their cousin Tim and second cousin Simon. They all got along and it was a friendly environment, but the collective nature of the management was stopping the business from moving forward. I realized that the older partners were not only confusing ownership with management, they were still doing the jobs of delivery boys. It looked to me as if it was time to look for a new boss from within the family.

Muncaster Castle, Cumbria

A beautiful stately home, Muncaster Castle had been in the Pennington family for centuries. Previously run by the formidable matriarch Phyllida Gordon-Duff-Pennington and her husband Patrick, and now nominally managed by their daughter Iona, the castle and grounds were open to the public, and this, together with Muncaster's use as a venue for weddings and the letting out of accommodation, provided significant income which was growing steadily. However, the castle was crumbling, the costs were escalating and it was necessary to attract 60,000 tourists each year just to break even. Iona and her husband Peter were due eventually to inherit the castle and – when they were not arguing – had some money-spinning ideas that could save their home. Unfortunately the older generation were resistant to change and had different ideas. The long-term future of the estate looked as if it could be in peril, and the idea of selling it was anathema to the family. It was a small group of people with opposing ideas, facing a financial crisis. My job was clear – to ensure the heiress took real charge sooner rather than later, and to explore which of her fresh ideas might work.

The Vernon Road Dyeing Factory, Nottingham

Richard Chaplin had bought a bankrupt lace-dyeing factory in Nottingham nine months before I arrived to help him. He had been managing director within his father, Henry's, previous firm before buying his own business, and Henry was now acting as chairman at Vernon Road. They had taken on the work-force of over a hundred at the same time, and staff relations were poor as the owners attempted to turn the business around as quickly as possible. Richard was a fearsome and exacting boss who employed his old friend and colleague Jeff Mason to motivate the work-force into working harder and more efficiently. It had the opposite effect. If the staff did not like and trust the management the company was doomed, so I needed to work on a two-pronged approach of improving staff morale and effecting changes at the top.

The Old Manor Hotel, Fife

Alistair Clark had been running this fiefdom in Fife for twelve years, and had turned in a profit every year since it opened. Although it was one of the most successful small hotels in Scotland, he was a tough, bullying and workaholic boss who struck fear into many who worked for him – including his two sons Michael and George. The boys thought they might one day inherit, but their father was keeping them at arm's length. He feared they might ruin the business, and the sons felt he would interfere with whatever they wanted to do. I had to find a way for Alistair to ease off and for the boys to gain enough confidence and experience to take the business on.

Norwood Park, Nottinghamshire

Sir John and Lady Starkey lived on this lovely 500-acre estate which had been in the Starkey family for 120 years. Over the past forty Sir John had been running three businesses (a golf course, a wedding business and a fruit farm), all of which, I was informed, had been successful. They had three daughters and one son, and the laws of primogeniture dictated that the estate should pass eventually to the son, Henry. Sir John was sixty-five and felt it was time to hand over the reins. He seemed to doubt that Henry was up to running the businesses (his wife expressed this doubt in stronger terms). Meanwhile at least one of the daughters was a possible contender for the job. After examining the figures, I could see that the estate was not in good shape financially. It needed a huge cash injection and it needed sound management. I knew what I wanted to do: turn tradition on its head and replace Henry with someone else. My worry was that this would be unacceptable to the family.

• Arrow Ford Car Dealership, Wales

This, one of the oldest Ford dealerships in South Wales, had once upon a time been a moderately successful business. Three years ago it turned over £5 million, but since then it had been steadily losing money. This was partly to do with the problems the car industry in general was facing, with margins being increasingly squeezed. But what was to my mind a deeper problem, was that managing director Robin Harris was fed up and morale throughout the company was low. He simply couldn't see a way to improve profits. Although he had two daughters working in the company, he deliberately kept them away from the management side. He held virtually no meetings, kept disappearing off on holiday and was vague about the true financial picture. I knew the success or failure of the business rested with the group of people who were there, and it was clear that in order to save it Robin should hand over to a better manager. I had a pretty shrewd idea who this manager might be: Nigel Bond, who ran one part of the business efficiently and profitably. My task, then, was to persuade Robin to give up his 'baby' and to hammer out a deal that would incentivize Nigel to rescue the entire business. If possible, I also wanted the daughters, Sam and Jo, to be more involved on the management side.

• County Linen, Essex

Established in 1815, this business had been in the Moore family for seven generations. With a staff of over 400 and customers that included the Savoy and the Houses of Parliament, it used to be highly profitable. Five years ago the business made a profit of £1 million, but last year it turned in a loss of £700,000. Father Dudley had been in charge for thirty years and was talking of retirement, so his sons Tim and Anthony had taken on the running of the two plants in Chelmsford and Clacton. When I arrived staff were unhappy, productivity was at an all-time low, customers were dissatisfied, Anthony and Tim were floundering, and no one seemed to know what to do to get the business back on its feet. My job was to get them all to look closely at what was going wrong, to sort out the leadership issues, and to see if Dudley could be encouraged to retire and then find a way of helping one of his sons to take proper control.

* * *

If you have picked up this book the chances are that you're in management, you want to go further, you want your business to have the success it deserves, and you may also have seen the TV series. Perhaps you are even involved in a family business. My aim and fervent hope is that reading this will enable you to look clearly at the challenges facing you at work and, almost as if an objective observer like myself were sitting next to you, to cut to the chase and find real workable solutions. It is a book about a variety of businesses that demonstrate management lessons for us all, and it is a book for you to use as a guide to those parts of your business life that could use some improvement. The lessons are applicable also to any organization or voluntary group, and even to your personal life. I should mention here that not all the companies featured in the TV series took my advice.

In the interests of simplicity I refer to managers throughout the book as 'he'. By this I mean absolutely no disrespect to women – in fact I am convinced that by the end of this century women will be the dominant force in business. (I only need to look at my daughters and their friends to know that this is true!)

I truly believe that good management is not rocket science. You don't need to be a genius, you don't need several letters after your name, you don't even need to be full of ideas. But you do need to be level-headed. I wanted to call this book 'Management Made Easy' (but someone had used that title already). I hope it makes it easy for you.

CHAPTER ONE

▶ Leadership

If you get the right person running something your problems are fundamentally solved

If there was an overarching theme to the *I'll Show Them Who's Boss* series, it was leadership. In the original *Troubleshooter* series Sir John Harvey-Jones concentrated on the nuts and bolts of companies in order to turn around their fortunes. In some cases it worked well, but if there's a fundamental problem with the conductor you will not solve the orchestra's woes by retuning the fifth violin. Likewise, if a business is underperforming then I'd bet my bottom dollar that you need look no further than the boss. I'll show you why in this chapter.

What kind of a person is a leader?

A leader is much more than just a figurehead. A leader is the person who makes the major decisions about where the business is going. The person who decides on the big issues, the issues that will make things happen that are different from the things that are happening now. This person needs to be someone with rather exceptional qualities – some of which can be learnt, but most of which are innate:

- ### That *je ne sais quoi*

In many ways it is really very difficult to define exactly what it is that makes someone a leader. To start with, I think the kernel of it is something that is either there or it's not: you're born with it. Some people can walk into a room and you immediately get a feeling about them. You subconsciously react to certain qualities in them. In the case of a strong leader you sense that this person has a self-belief, a security about himself. Leaders know what they're doing; they have an aura of authority. It's partly charisma, partly a comfort factor. You are comforted, not in some soft cuddly way but by a sense of being in safe hands, of being with someone who will take care of things in the right way at the right time. It may be very subtle, but it is always there.

● Nous

In Henry's hands it would collapse
a bit. Quite a lot, actually
VICTORIA STARKEY, Norwood Park

This is rather hard to put your finger on too. It's not academic intelligence; it has got nothing to do with business experience, although both of these may help. Rather it is a kind of acumen, a realism, an in-touch-with-the-world-ness, a finely honed intuitive sense. I've seen many very clever people intellectualize a business to death, while on the other hand many highly successful business leaders and entrepreneurs are the bunk-off-school, raid-the-sweet-shop types who survive on native wit and cunning. I'm a great believer in the fact that someone who has run a business for thirty years is far more useful than someone who has spent the last five at Harvard. Good gut instinct is worth a fortune.

My wife does the kitchen and I,
er, I run the, er, business
HENRY STARKEY, Norwood Park

● Clarity

A leader needs to be crystal clear on what the issues are and on exactly where the company is headed. Too often people in leadership positions are muddled about where they want to get to.

Part of what a leader does is take complex issues, break them down and lay them out in a way that is easy to understand. This analytical capacity is crucial and needs to be accompanied by a strong desire to simplify things rather than complicate them. It is, in a way, a scientific quality, a capacity to make a true and objective observation of what is actually there rather than some preconception of what you would like it to be. I cannot emphasize this enough, because our capacity to see what we want to see is nothing short of awesome. You must fight it all the time, because it is extremely difficult to get from A to B if you're kidding yourself that you're starting from C.

Not only does a leader need to see clearly and objectively, he needs to be direct and straight in the way he communicates with his people. It is extremely boring and very irritating to work with someone who goes round the houses to get anything done. It is a killer. It is crucial to convey an issue so that, as a result of seeing what it is, people can buy into and accept it, and go forward. Lack of clarity is a particular problem in family businesses and in businesses where the market-place is changing. I'll go into this topic further in Chapter 6.

Vision

If you haven't got an objective, get one! Define what it is you're aiming to do – and don't waffle. Surprisingly, this most crucial issue in leading a company forward is often forgotten. Your objective should tread that fine line between being something that is stretching and something that is do-able. If it is impossible it demotivates people. If it is too easy it demotivates people. A good leader's ambition for the company is nearly always beyond what most people think is possible, but you as leader must have a real sense that it is possible – and this involves good judgement. Each industry is different and it is the leader's responsibility to set an appropriate, challenging target for everyone in the business to aim at. For more on developing a vision and strategy see Chapter 2.

Passion

My head is going to explode if
I can't run this thing
SIMON, George Brown & Sons

This is an interesting one. Firstly, you really have to have the passion to lead, otherwise you simply won't be able to deal with the stress levels, and when the going gets tough your people will see through you. Secondly, to succeed you absolutely have to have a real passion for the business you are in. But a word of warning: passion by itself is not enough. Passion in the hands of those who lack judgement is the most dangerous thing I have ever come across, and it is far better to do nothing with a business than to lead it passionately down the wrong path. Before you unleash your passion, do your homework, use your nous, examine carefully. I'm not saying you have to get everything absolutely right, but you must be on the right track. Your passion must be aimed at a target that makes sense. Study the business pages of the quality dailes for a few weeks to find many examples of misdirected passion.

Remember the cautionary tale of Marconi, a hugely successful company when run by Lord Weinstock. He ran a very tight ship, was perhaps even a little overcautious, but he had, during his stewardship, built up a company of enormous value. When he retired his successor George Simpson, who had energy and dynamism and no doubt a great deal of passion, bought several software and telecom companies to use up the accumulated cash. Gone were the old cautious, slow-moving ways! Sadly in his passion and enthusiasm he overpaid – and blew Marconi apart within five years. A similar disaster was perpetrated by Graham Wallace at Cable & Wireless. The dotcom fiasco is yet another object lesson in passion gone mad. Wild sums of money were thrown at ill-thought-through ideas that were simply not grounded in reality. It always looked ridiculous to me: I could never see how these enterprises, often valued at a billion pounds, were going to create genuine profits and cash. Yet the illusion went on and on, with business leaders and financiers chucking good money after bad. Hitler was passionate, so be warned!

● Courage

People see somebody with a suit on
and think, 'Cor, he's got it made,'
but they don't realize just how much
mental work and dedication it takes
DAVID BROWN, George Brown & Sons

I think running a business is quite frightening. You have to stick your neck out, take risks, and put yourself on the line. Often it is your own money and your family's future you have at stake. It's definitely not for the faint-hearted – real courage is required. On the other hand I have worked with people who refuse to take any risks at all, people who insist on analysing everything to death and then end up making no decisions because they are afraid of getting it wrong. This leads to huge demotivation and stagnation. Do your analysis and research, of course, but, once you have marshalled your facts, apply your judgement and 'nous', and get on with it. If it becomes clear that you have got it wrong, then again you need the courage to stop it in its tracks. Often this takes the greatest courage of all, because it means you have to admit that you've made a mistake: never easy. But if you don't take risks, you won't get huge payouts.

Clearly there needs to be a balance between being courageous and being downright foolhardy. I took a big risk when I joined Granada as chief executive. Granada was considered a 'basket case' at the time. As it turned out this was unfair, because Alex Bernstein had already achieved a great deal in getting it back on track. However, there was still a lot to do. Perhaps the most courageous thing I did was to sack David Plowright, chief executive of Granada Television, who felt that he could carry on as before and ignore the changes that were essential to the success of the company. He had been there for many years and – something I failed to appreciate fully – had a great deal of support among staff and the TV stars themselves. He simply didn't believe he could be removed, and when he was an enormous media storm blew up, and it took months for the adverse publicity to die down. Perhaps if I had been aware of the storm it would cause I might have found some way to sideline him, rather than sack him. However, I am glad I had the nerve to do what I did, because Granada TV went from strength to strength. The hostile bid for Trust House Forte was also pushing the courage envelope: it was risky to go after a company that theoretically had a device to stop a predatory takeover. The Council of Forte had voting rights over more than 50 per cent of the shares and could have stopped the bid. It says a great deal about the honour and decency of Rocco Forte that he never attempted to use them. By that time Granada had a large presence in the hospitality and catering sector, so I knew many parts of his business well; every time we came up against these we could see how much better we ourselves were doing at the same thing. We compared their operations with ours, and found that in our central office we employed a tenth of the people they did in theirs; we interviewed disaffected staff, so we understood the issues and pressures; we visited each location ... We basically went to town on finding out as much as we could. The upshot was that we had a strong feeling that there were things we could do better, and the judgement we then had to make was simply how much better we could do than they were doing. On top of that I spent a lot of time studying Rocco himself, to see how he operated and how he was regarded by his staff and shareholders. In the end, however, you never know it all and you have to muster the courage to take the plunge.

It seems to me that courage in leadership is also about having the strength and enterprise to be able to see a different future for the company, and not simply a running-on of what has happened in the past. I've seen many situations where everyone has said, 'It's hopeless, it just can't be done,' and then someone new comes in, sees a way forward, and takes everyone with him. Things that seemed impossible start to fall away, and the very same people who thought it was impossible realize they can go on to achieve something special. In a way this harks back to my point about vision and clarity, but it is also about being brave enough to go for it.

As long as I'm here I'd want to be involved in it
ALISTAIR CLARK, The Old Manor Hotel

Before I leave this topic, a word about handling the isolating experience that is leadership. There is no doubt that it is lonely at the top. You need inner resilience and courage for this too. No longer can you be one of the lads, no longer can you confide in people you might have regarded as your friends in a previous job. They don't want you to and they won't let you, and you shouldn't anyway: you can't be all that chummy and cosy when you expect results. My first taste of this came when I was promoted from sales and marketing director at Grand Met's Coca-Cola franchise to become MD of the whole soft drinks operation. It was tough. I have talked to many people about this, and it seems to be the same for them. So either you have to like being by yourself, or you must be absolutely clear that you'll have to do things outside your work to fulfil your need for collegiate activity. Business isn't that important, it really isn't. After all, life should be made up of many elements: work, family, home, friends, holidays, keeping healthy and so on. Make sure you have it in balance: what is crucial is being a rounded individual, which means getting away and having nothing to do with work for reasonable periods of time – at least for weekends, if not longer. If you can't do this I think you're just kidding yourself. The real truth is, if your business is properly set up it can run without you. Even when I was in full-time employment it was pretty rare for me to be there on Friday afternoons. Unless there was a takeover or something going on, I would switch off completely, particularly if I could absorb myself in one of my hobbies such as painting, playing golf or skiing. And I'd always leave firm instructions that I was not to be disturbed. It's so important today, with mobile phones and e-mail, that we learn to make demarcations between work life and home life. Don't allow yourself to be crushed by the whole thing. This too requires courage, because it's easier to pretend that you are indispensable. You're not.

It can be very lonely running a business. You can't always talk to the family about everything because you don't want to upset them
ROBIN HARRIS, Arrow Ford

● Rallying the troops

If you can't rally the troops, then you're not a leader. For some it's a kind of showbiz thing, an ability to tell your people that you're all in it together, you're doing an exciting thing, and make them feel that they'd rather be here than anywhere else. What's more important, perhaps, is that they feel you are being fair and reasonable in the hard work that you are asking of them, that the company is doing good things and that you will all succeed together. People actually do want to be led, they want to respect the leader and they need to feel excited about the future of what it is they are doing. This ability to inspire and to motivate is very powerful – think Winston Churchill: 'We will fight them on the beaches', think Shakespeare's Henry V at Agincourt, and you'll know what I mean. It's great if you can do it, but it's not the only way. If you are the type who can make a big splash at major events such as sales conferences, annual meetings and results announcements, fantastic. These occasions are a good opportunity to have a party and to do your rousing backslapping spiel, and it's all very good for morale. I believe, however, that 'rallying' can also, paradoxically, be an individual, quiet thing. I'm thinking of those one-to-one opportunities you get every day for encouragement, for conveying your passion about the business – about one single idea even – to the person you happen to be with at that moment. Your aim should be to leave everyone you talk to feeling good about their particular projects, and great about the part they play in the business as a whole. This is particularly important – even vital – in your dealings with those individuals who report directly to you. Your enthusiasm and belief in them will act as a rallying call that will be heard throughout the organization. The attitudes and behaviour of a leader eventually permeate the entire company.

● Consistency

*It is so unstable, there is something
different every day*
FACTORY WORKER, Vernon Road

*You do exactly what you said you're
going to do at the rate you've said
you're going to do it, and that's it*
NIGEL BOND, Arrow Ford

Follow-up
This is a much underrated facet of good leadership, and is definitely something that can be learnt. If you say you are going to do something, do it. If you ask for something to be done, check that it has been. If you don't, people are unnerved the first time, and by the second and third times they will know that they can get away with not doing it. This is the road to failure.

For example, if you agree with the sales manager that by next month he will need only two people on the sales team and not three, think about what happens if next month you forget to ask about this. The sales manager, if he hasn't done it, is relieved but unsettled. If he has, he has just carried out a very difficult task but now he feels you haven't noticed, and he's even more unsettled. He will think twice in future about whether he actually has to carry out what you ask him to do. Follow-up is essential, but don't panic. You don't need an elephant's memory (I have a terrible one); you need a good system. This is something that I learnt many years ago from Alan Costin, who was my boss at Lex Service Group. This is it:

- Make sure your meetings for the whole year are mapped out. They should be held at least once a month with every person who reports directly to you. Stick to them religiously.
- During the meeting, take brief but clear notes.
- After the meeting, type them up and send them to the person with whom you held the meeting, specifying what is to be done, by whom and by when.
- Next time you meet, have the memo on the table as a checklist of what should have happened.

It's so obvious, so simple, and it works at any level, whether your subordinate is painting the lines in the car park or in charge of launching a new product. The beauty of it is that you both know that things will not go away or get lost or forgotten – there will be follow-up. When I worked for Anthony Tennant at Grand Met, who operated a similar system, I would spend about an hour a month with him, after which I would hardly see him until the next meeting. But I knew that when he asked me for something I jolly well did it. With this system there is no escape, no getting away from tasks, and also, in a very positive way, there is a regular chance for the leader to give praise for a job well done. In addition, you should keep a file in your desk for each individual. As you pass things to him or her for attention or action, pop a copy in the file, which you then run through with them at your regular monthly review to ensure that it has been observed or acted upon.

What sort of mood is he in today?

One day he'll be friendly;
another day he won't talk
VICTORIA, The Old Manor Hotel

Your people must know how they will find you. Don't be friendly and positive one moment, unpleasant and irritable the next. It is terribly important to behave in a consistent manner. People must be sure that they will find you in a particular mood, even if it is dour and miserable! Whether you are taking someone to task for their poor performance or praising them, your style should be exactly the same. So if you are someone who is up on some days and down on others, or if your mood tends to be affected, for example, by the weekly sales figures, you should very consciously try to make your style consistent. It can be hard, especially if there are business difficulties, but if you are unpredictable you will be frightening to deal with. Take control of your reactions, relax, and strive to be level-headed, honest and decent in your dealings. Never make a people decision when you're angry. It is possible to rule by fear, but a bit of decency goes a long way.

Be consistent in your objectives for the company
This is absolutely vital. Stick to what you say the company is going to do. Don't keep changing your mind; allow things to progress for a reasonable time along a certain path, so that staff are confident that management is in control and has a firm hand on the tiller. People need to feel confident that what the business is doing is consistent. It is very disturbing for staff if you're sending them round collecting information, doing projects, assessing new markets, researching ideas and so on, then a little further down the line you do a U-turn and dispatch them in other directions. Organizations flounder and sway a great deal more under this kind of leadership than is generally appreciated, and it is a block to effective progress. Of course, if it is clear that you are really going wrong, don't be afraid to admit it and change things. Just be absolutely sure of your facts. If you are not going to do something, then don't waste people's time researching it. Have the courage to say no at the beginning.

Don't try to do too many things

Keep it simple or you risk losing that crucial clarity of vision. A leader's job is to be brilliant at a few big things. Be consistent in the tasks you set for yourself, and keep your eye on the ball. Let others deal with the detail. If you jump in and attempt to solve everyone's problems unasked, you not only risk making more mistakes, but you'll lose your focus and undermine your staff by never giving them a chance to think and act for themselves. Of course, when people do ask for help, take time to understand the issues and ask intelligent questions to highlight the best way forward.

● Talent-spotting and delegating

Because you should not attempt to do everything as a leader, you need good people around you. Some of these will be people with their own leadership potential, and it is important to be able to spot them. Don't be afraid of strong characters coming up through the ranks – in fact, you should encourage this because it is important for the future health of the business. Structure your business so that they have opportunities to shine, develop their careers and become good leaders for the people who report to them. I have a theory that while people of great ability often don't reach the top, it is pretty rare for people with no ability to get through: they get rumbled on the way. Remember it is your job to nurture that upcoming pool of talent.

Effective delegating is essential for you to clear your own mind (and desk) and to encourage others. What you need to do is:

- Decide straight away whether it is something for you to deal with yourself, or whether it is a task that someone else is capable of handling. (A first-class PA will stop most stuff coming to your desk in the first place.)
- If it is the latter (and you should try hard to make it so), make sure you set the outcome, rather than the method, when you pass it on. Specify the end result you want and fight very hard against telling the person how to do the task. If you dictate their every move you will never discover whether they are capable of running anything.
- Trust your subordinates to bring in their own people, make their own decisions and take their own risks – obviously staying within the broad

bounds of what you want to happen.
- Be prepared to put serious effort into encouraging them on their path.

The great thing about this approach is that you can encourage distinct pockets of creativity. If there is a new venture or market to be tested, give someone the chance by investing in a pilot scheme. In almost every business there are opportunities that are not being fully exploited in some way, and often those who are closer to the ground will have a strong feeling of what these could be. It is incredibly motivating for someone to be given the chance to grow the business and develop their career in this way, and, more important, it also leaves you free to concentrate on those elusive big issues.

So it is all these qualities that, for me, represent the key things you should be aiming for if you are a leader, if you are hoping one day to run something, or if you are looking for someone to take over the running of your business. Some people are born with many of these skills, but they often go unrecognized and are therefore undeveloped. You really can acquire them with determination, commitment and self-belief. But there's something else, which isn't always obvious:

Singularity (the buck stops here)

In ten years no one has sat down
and said, 'Pick somebody, put them
at the top, and the rest of you
guys cover the flanks'
ALLAN McCALLUM-TOPPIN, AMT Espresso

If you have watched some of the *I'll Show Them Who's Boss* episodes you can't fail to have noticed me banging on about one particular aspect of leadership: singularity. By that I mean having just one leader. Almost without exception the businesses I looked at had failed to face this issue head-on, because it was difficult for all sorts of non-business reasons. I tried, often in a hard-nosed way, to force them to face up to it. One person has to have the final say. It's as crude as that. After all, you wouldn't get on a plane or ship that lacked a captain who could lay down the law in moments of crisis, and it's the same in business for three major reasons:

*Who actually is the boss? We haven't
really got one. We are left to our
own devices*
WORKER, County Linen

Clarity (again!)
Many people like to think they have a say in what happens, and more often than not they think the best way to do this is to be involved in every major decision. Actually life is simpler, clearer and better for the company and the individuals in it if there is complete agreement that there is one person running it. The businesses that lacked singularity of leadership fuddled and muddled their way through meetings with very little being decided. Hopeless! What you need is one authoritative leader who makes decisions, so that there is no confusion, no ambiguity, no uncertainty, and everyone can get on knowing that they're all facing in the same direction. A fudge is no good at all, and on serious issues can be downright disastrous.

*I just wanna do what it takes to move
forward and stop messing around*
ALASTAIR MCCALLUM-TOPPIN, AMT Espresso

Rapidity

*I'm excited for the first time in years
that perhaps we can go somewhere*
SAM, Arrow Ford

Where decisions are made by consensus, things happen much more slowly and, frankly, business is not an area where slowness pays off. There are times when you simply have to have the flexibility to move very quickly indeed, and for this a single leader is essential. People who have been enormously successful in complex industries have usually achieved what they have because of their quick reaction times. Part of Sky TV's strength, for example, is that Tom Bell and Rupert Murdoch are prepared to take a decision on the spot. Many organizations go through an endless process of meetings and complex approval structures before they begin to make a decision. If they're family businesses, they often go all over the place. While this tortuous system follows its course, somebody else is saying, 'Come on – let's do this,' and the market moves on. Equally important, if you need to reverse a mistake that has been made, the business may be haemorrhaging money before the decision to do this is eventually taken. In family firms without strong leadership, where things have been done a certain way for years, this makes them acutely vulnerable. In most areas of commerce, the market-place has been changing more quickly over the past ten years than it has over the past fifty, so there is a real danger that if businesses cannot be nimble on their feet they will soon become obsolete. One strong leader can change this.

Comfort

People do not spend their days thinking about the person who leads the organization unless it is all going horribly wrong. However, having a distant, approving, authoritative leader in the background lends a sense of order and calm to an organization. It's rather like when you were in your bedroom as a child, with your mum and/or dad in the house – a sense of calm, a feeling that someone is control, and that everything will be all right. Distance often helps too – we need a little sense of mystery that someone 'up there' is dealing with the difficult, unpredictable things in life, making everything safe. Have you noticed how worries and concerns can miraculously disappear once you have discussed them with your boss? This sense of comfort and stability is only achievable with singularity.

Leadership and ownership

Ownership of a business is not the same as leadership of a business. It can be, of course – some owners want to run the show even if others do not. Those who do want to run it need to be very careful because, as we saw time and again in *I'll Show Them Who's Boss*, people with the money to buy businesses, or people who inherit businesses, do not necessarily have the ability to lead them. In most organizations, people work their way up into managerial positions because they have the capacity to lead, and a selection process has been going on. They are generally there because they have proved that they can lead. The trouble with ownership is that it can cut across that kind of ability. We know now the kind of qualities a leader has. A good owner on the other hand has rather different qualities: he needs to be thoughtful, kind, trustworthy and reasonable, and has to be able to see the big picture. He may also need deep pockets! An owner can have some control over the major decisions as a shareholder, but if he has appointed a management team he should not be involved in the day-to-day running of the company.

This becomes a very interesting and complex issue in the case of family businesses, which often tend to be passed down to the 'next person in line'. What is often not appreciated, until it is too late, is that a business can be enormously successful without a single member of the family running it (think of Granada or Tesco, for instance). Indeed, in my view, for a company to continue to be healthy over a long period of time there comes a point where it is essential for ownership and leadership to separate. The joint-stock company is a marvellous vehicle and it has pretty well become the entity on which all our commercial lives are based. For in it you have a vehicle which separates ownership from management. If you think about it, if you give yourself one or two people from whom to choose a leader, things are almost bound to go wrong. You have to go outside, and this is the reason why very small businesses rarely survive beyond the third or fourth generation with family members running them. See Chapter 7 for more on the mess that family- and owner-run businesses can get themselves into.

Structuring an organization for effective leadership

In order to see where you fit into your organization, where you would like to aim for, or how you could restructure your company if necessary, here is a brief look at the best structure for an organization. Obviously it depends on how large the company is, and if you are very small the bedrock should be a managing director and a financial director. If you need to downsize, start with human resources and strategy and continue from there. Any director should have a maximum of seven people reporting to him; any more and it is impossible to be a friend, a motivator, a demanding taskmaster and all the other things a boss has to be.

CHAIRMAN

A chairman (usually part-time) leads the board and is responsible to the shareholders/owners. He is there to ensure good corporate governance and to be a uniting force for the company. He should be forward-looking and imaginative, and should assess the performance and calibre of those executives just below board level. His principal job, however, is to motivate, lead and support the chief executive and to remove and replace him in the event of his failure. He must stand back from the day-to-day running of the company.

A past chief executive of the company may become chairman, and an owner of a company can be a chairman, although it is often better for the sake of objectivity for an outsider to be brought in. In some companies the roles of chief executive and chairman are successfully combined, but I believe the two are best separated.

NON-EXECUTIVE DIRECTORS

A medium–sized company will have three or four non-executive directors who watch the performance of the company and check that the main board is operating correctly. It helps if they have some particular field of expertise such as legal knowledge, a financial qualification, or useful connections. You do not often find them in a family business, although ironically they could bring some much-needed (non-family) balance to the behaviour of the executives in such companies. The chairman and the non-executive directors meet with the executive directors at a board meeting between six and ten times a year. They report to the chairman of the company but should have a good relationship with the chief executive.

CHIEF EXECUTIVE

Sometimes called managing director, this is the person we have been talking about in this chapter – a good, strong business leader, responsible for seeing that the business is running well. Along with the other directors (see below) he is responsible to the chairman and board, and usually sends a report (or gives a presentation) to the board in advance of the monthly meetings.

OTHER DIRECTORS

Reporting to the chief executive, these should always include:

Finance director

and sometimes, depending on the size and type of the business,

Marketing director
Creative director
New product development director
Sales director
Production director
Human resources director

SENIOR MANAGEMENT

The next tier of management, reporting directly to the various directors.

Let's look now at how some of the businesses I advised for *I'll Show Them Who's Boss* were led in terms of personalities and leadership potential. In the next chapter we will look at their business strategies: leadership in action.

AMT Espresso The first thing I did was to sit in as an observer at one of the brothers' meetings. I sat and watched the three of them (Angus, Allan and Alastair) argue for nearly an hour over details such as the taste of the flapjacks and colour of the coffee cups. I was concerned not only that they were ignoring the big issues such as marketing, financing, expansion and so on, but also by the antagonism between them. It was immediately obvious that one of the brothers needed to step ahead of the others and be the leader, but which one? The oldest and the youngest disagreed and contradicted each other regularly, while the middle one played piggy in the middle. None of the brothers had the upper hand, yet they all wanted to make decisions, and as a result nothing much was being decided. The company had grown quickly, but it was operating in a highly competitive industry and was beginning to get to a size where management skills were going to be necessary. The brothers needed to sharpen up their act if it was to maintain its successful position. They admitted that they were very unhappy about the way that they worked together. They knew that this was no way to run a growing business. I needed to get to know them better and talk to them individually about how each saw the company's future.

It emerged that the youngest brother, Alastair, clearly felt he was the boss, and behaved accordingly. He had without doubt the most drive, passion and energy of the three, but something told me he did not at that stage have the skills necessary to be an effective leader. He appeared arrogant and lacking in maturity, and while I could see him running the show in perhaps five to ten years' time, I was uncomfortable about putting him in the top position at this point. Angus, the oldest brother, was enormously talented but quietly destructive in his style. He was skilled at dealing with the suppliers, but I felt he wouldn't make it as a boss. That left Allan: the quiet one, the peacemaker. I was impressed by his awareness of the human dynamics around the three of them, and how they operated (or rather didn't), and I had a strong feeling that he had in fact been running the company more than he realized (he referred to himself as the 'bomb diffuser', or the 'referee'), but he was sure that Alastair was a natural-born leader. That may have been so, but not at that point. Allan had a greater maturity and, I felt, a clearer vision of where the company was headed. So I suggested the job be given to Allan. This, I was convinced, would have ensured the future success of the company, but the brothers could not accept this undermining of Alastair's authority, and later in the story we were asked to stop filming.

* * *

George Brown & Sons, the fruit and vegetable delivery company, was also run on a 'we all do it together' basis, although they were much friendlier towards each other than the AMT brothers. I realized that the three older partners, who owned the company, felt they ought to be the managers (a classic confusion, as we have seen), but what they were really doing, in many ways because they were comfortable with it, and because they enjoyed it, was driving the delivery lorries. So while they were out on the road no single person was acting as leader: no one was taking responsibility for assessing effectiveness of deliveries, setting up new sales initiatives, exploring new markets, weeding out the bad customers from the good, and so on. The market was changing quickly, with the supermarkets doing their own buying direct from growers and the catering trade heading down much the same road as the supermarkets.

The partners felt it wasn't perfect, but it worked well enough. It wasn't working, though, because they were losing money and it was getting worse. In fact it was a disaster waiting to happen. The company clearly needed strong leadership to keep it from going under, so I decided to stir things up and throw the floor open to anyone from any generation and from any branch of the family who thought they had what it took to be the boss. Again I interviewed everyone personally, asking for their thoughts on how they would take the business forward if they were given the leading role. I was very impressed, not only by how nice they all were but by the number of talented people around, in sales, processing and administration. They cared deeply about the firm, and there were strong family bonds. Many of them were buzzing with ideas for the future, and you can read about their individual presentations in the next chapter. These helped me form a sense of how they would perform as leaders too, but in terms of who had the right qualities to make it as a leader, I gleaned the following mostly from the interviews.

David, one of the three owners, who was outwardly the most obvious contender, was simply not interested. I suspect he felt too old, did not want the hassle of running the company, and was low on ideas and drive. Jim, his cousin, was only really interested in sales, and although he had some clear ideas about what could be done to maximize efficiency in his own area he was lacking in vision for the company as a whole. Paul, David's brother and the third owner, was solid and dependable, and would agree to take on the leadership if he had to, but I could see there was little drive there. Paul's eldest daughter Lorraine, on the other hand, was very good on the issues facing the company and on what could be done to maximize profit in the future. I was a little concerned about her self-deprecating style, and the fact that she tended to talk her way around issues before reaching the point. Although she had the ideas and 'nous', and was clearly an organized, efficient person, she did not strike me immediately as being strong enough on confidence and clarity of communication. Her sister Ruth admitted that she felt years away from being ready to run the operation, but she did have a good sense of people's individual talents. Their brother Philip was great on the operational side, but lacked a helicopter vision of the company. Cousin Tim was good on the cold-calling side, but could not really think ahead on other issues. Finally, it was Simon, Jim's son, who really hit the jackpot for me. Not only was his presentation clear, sensible and refreshing, but he also left me in no doubt that he really, really wanted to lead the company. What's more, his approach was inclusive: he could see real roles that played to the strengths of other members of the family. He did not beat about the bush as the others had done. His only fear was that he would be seen as too young, too radical, too full of new ideas.

The old guard, as often happens, were deeply unsettled by the idea of someone from the younger generation coming in over their heads to run the company, and decided in my absence to appoint Paul as leader. This, to my mind, was the kiss of death for the company. People hate change and there was a recognition that with Paul there would be little change – yet change was what was needed. What's good for a company is not always good for people's comfort zones! I eventually persuaded them to give Simon a chance, and under his dynamic management the company has been going from strength to strength. He concentrated on the catering trade only, and sales increased by virtue of a dedicated sales team. Costs were cut by buying directly from the growers and by taking the expensive partners off the road; there was an image overhaul with a more 'branded' look, and personnel were shifted around to ensure that the right people were in the right jobs. A year later they were £50,000 in profit – the best results for fifteen years – and on target for a 25 per cent increase for the following year. With this track record, Simon and Lorraine were able to raise money to buy out the three owners little more than a year after Simon's takeover as managing director. This was a smart move – there is a lot to be said for finding a route to start afresh like this. And so the process starts again with new owners. Nice and simple.

* * *

Lack of one authoritative leader was also holding back the Duff-Penningtons of **Muncaster Castle**: they needed to make up their minds who was running the business. There was a classic muddle going on, which was leading to frustration for everyone and a long-term threat to the castle's fortunes. Phyllida, who owned the castle and had run it with her husband for years, and who was now seventy-four, felt she wasn't being told what was going on and continued to try to exert control. But when questioned she stated that her husband Patrick was really in charge. Patrick admitted in private that while their daughter Iona was nominally in control, in fact Phyllida continued as though she were in charge. Meanwhile, Iona felt she was in charge and could do well at it if given space to do so. Her husband Peter felt blocked by both these strong women. Are you with me still? That there was a terrific battle of wills going on was clear to me when I sat in on their meetings and noticed how Phyllida did exercise very strong control even when she said nothing. I could tell by her eloquent silences that she was thinking, 'I don't agree, this isn't right, we shouldn't be doing this – in fact we shouldn't even be discussing it.' Phyllida's power of veto was holding them back.

Meanwhile Iona and Peter were itching to get on with modernizing the business. In most organizations there would have been a vote by this point, and the chairman's period of office would be over. In this family (as in many family businesses) there was no mechanism for allowing this to happen, largely because no one wanted to hurt Phyllida. Things had to move on; the castle needed to attract more visitors and redevelop parts of the estate to maximize earnings potential. It was obvious to me that Iona should be left to lead the business: she had passion, good ideas and ability, and it would eventually be hers anyway. The problem I had was how to tread carefully enough over family sensibilities to ensure that everyone was eventually happy with this solution.

Two years on, under Iona's passionate and focused leadership the castle has had its most successful year ever. Muncaster won the prestigious title of 'Best Visitor Attraction in England' in 2003; forty 'ghost-sits' have been held; two accommodation units have been completed; they are developing the 'world's best owl centre'; visitor numbers are up to 80,000; and they are introducing a new lighting scheme and interactive computers. Staff are motivated and happy, and, according to Peter, Phyllida is kept informed but maintains a discreet distance. Although they say they have a long way to go, they are getting on with it.

* * *

At the **Vernon Road Dyeing Factory** Richard Chaplin had unshakeable passion and belief in what he was doing, but he also had a major problem. He was inconsistent in his manner and inconsistent in what he was saying about his plans for the company ... and he was often blind to the effect that he had on people and the way he frightened them. I knew that unless he could recognize this and do something about it the business as it stood was doomed. He also seemed to believe that some of the work-force were the 'enemy', out to thwart what he was trying to do. Yet he was shocked when I explained how he came across. At some points during my involvement with his business he did seem to change – he stood up and made an impassioned speech about the future of the company and did his best to get the workers on side. His wife, endearingly, bought him a lilac shirt to reflect the 'new, softer Richard'. But his actions totally contradicted what he said, and the workers simply did not trust him. He promised that there would be only one round of redundancies, and there were more. He sacked the unpopular factory manager, and then re-employed him. If this wasn't inconsistency, I don't know what is. It was clear that he would never turn the company round if he was unable to change on this most fundamental point. After some time it was equally clear that he was not going to change, and I not-so-subtly told him that he needed to step down.

Some months after the camera crew left I did hear that Richard had eventually taken my advice and brought in a new management team. Jeff

Mason left to work for a rival. The work-force was reduced to forty-five, and pay was slashed. The factory continued to produce work for high street stores and famous-name labels, but additionally branched out into supplying textiles for cars, prisons, schools and the police force. However, I was sorry to read an article in late 2003 reporting that the company was going into receivership.

* * *

Sir John Starkey of **Norwood Park**, polymath and outwardly successful businessman, needed to hand his business over to younger hands. His only son Henry was due to become the fourth baronet of Norwood Park, which entailed inheriting the estate and the three businesses connected with it. As a small test, he and his wife had been given the golf-course business to run. He was a likeable chap, but there was a woolliness about him – he wasn't exactly sure what it was he was meant to be doing, and I had a sense that he was protesting too much, constantly reiterating that he really was going to succeed. 'I'll prove it,' he kept saying, which to me spoke of a terrible inner doubt. He simply didn't come across as a person who had enough of those special characteristics of a leader – he certainly had no business experience and had very little grasp of numbers and what they meant. My worry, however, was that he did have some of the characteristics: he was certainly passionate about the estate and wanted to do well – a potentially fatal combination – and he had already made some obvious mistakes on the golf side. If this were a non-family situation it would be instantly solvable – Henry would simply not be offered the top job. The problem was how to remove him from the top position without upsetting the family. It might be possible to carve up the business, with separate heads of each unit, but it was going to be essential to create a system which came to one single head. His elder sister Suzannah was married to a successful businessman, and between them they had the passion, vision and ability (and cash) to drive the business forward in a practical and profitable way. Despite this, and my valiant efforts to persuade Sir John of the very real benefits of choosing the best person for the job, he gave it to Henry – as I had always feared he would. At least the situation has been resolved and clarified (even if I disagreed with the outcome), and as long as Henry takes my advice about separating ownership from management and brings in an experienced business manager he may yet save the family home for future generations.

Robin Harris, managing director of the **Arrow Ford** car dealership, was in trouble. He was fundamentally not cut out to be a day-to-day leader; I felt he would have made a great salesman, trader or deal-maker instead. On a personal level I liked him very much, and I felt sorry for him. He was in a complete muddle about how the business was doing and where it should be going, he avoided getting involved in financial detail, he was not good at communication, and he rarely praised his staff. He had the air of a defeated man, and did not seem to be in a good shape to resurrect a business. As we know, if you haven't got a leader who is on sparkling form, you are in trouble. His two daughters seemed to be keen and capable, but he had kept them so far away from management positions that they were not ready for leadership. However, there was someone I had my eye on. Nigel Bond was the manager of the 'Rapid Fit' part of the business and an old friend of Robin's. He was ambitious and driven, was terrific at motivating people, and turned in good profits. He was intuitive, organized, and had a long-term attitude that involved squeezing every drop of business out of each customer. ('I ring and I beg for work when the place is absolutely crammed full,' he said.) It was tough, but I needed to speak frankly to Robin about what I saw as the only way forward. Hearing that my advice was for him to give up his job was not what he had expected when he invited me and the cameras into his business, and he fought valiantly and doggedly on nearly every point. Eventually I was able to broker a deal between the two men which was attractive enough to both, and in which Robin would become chairman and Nigel would take on the day-to-day running as managing director. The wonderful thing to see was that as soon as the deal was done, as Nigel said: 'Things changed dramatically. There is a far more positive attitude. We're really up and going for it. No matter what I ask for I get it immediately. Everybody is driving and pushing along with me, which is brilliant.' As far as the future goes, I can see Robin being a decent and hands-off joint owner, particularly as he has already started up a new property business.

* * *

Alistair Clark, managing director of **The Old Manor Hotel**, Fife, was a successful businessman, but his behaviour sometimes fell short of my requirements for good leadership. Yes, he had nous, sound judgement, vision, passion and courage. But often people didn't like him. He was something of a bully, he intimidated some of the staff, was obsessed with detail, and hardly ever went home. He would wake up in the night and add items to his 'to do' list. This kind of behaviour can be one of the downsides to people with incredible drive. 'What I don't like are slackers,' he asserted. On another occasion, a member of staff commented, 'There's usually a lot of swearing goes on if something gets done wrong. I guess that's what bosses are there for.' Alistair's two sons, Michael and George, due in time to inherit the business, were frightened of putting a foot wrong and in many ways were held back by him. I felt they were more than capable of taking the business on if only I could persuade Alistair to hand over. They seemed to have complementary skills (George had a background in finance; Michael was a former chef), and were happy with the idea of one of them (George) being the top dog. Alistair was deeply suspicious of their commitment to the company, and even when one of them moved house to be closer to the hotel it was still not enough for him. The brothers had presented to me what was an extremely impressive and well-thought-through strategic plan. Intellectually, they were up to the job, but as their father commented, 'Can they actually make it happen?' Sure enough, when I returned a few weeks later to check progress on the new plans I discovered that nothing had happened. The wonderful strategy document was tucked away in a drawer: they had fallen at the first hurdle. Was this because Alistair had never made them feel that they were capable? One of the single most important aspects of leadership is an ability to get on and do things, rather than simply thinking about them. So I put a bomb under the brothers and got things moving again. Another spur to action was provided by Alistair's agreeing to give George and Michael over 50 per cent of the company. This tremendously significant act not only gave them power and control, but represented the acknowledgement of trust that had for so long been missing. It took them a while to clock this, but finally they were genuinely fired up by the challenge of leadership.

* * *

One of the most obvious problems at **County Linen** was that there was no one single leader. Worse, it seemed to me that both Tim and Anthony Moore were totally lacking in enthusiasm for the business although Anthony was intelligent and personable. Tim, whom I liked very much, was depressed following a tragic event in his personal life and was clearly not cut out to be a business manager. There was a dreadful sense of duty and guilt weighing both of them down, and a fear that it would all fall apart 'on their shift'. Neither of them, at first, seemed to have the requisite passion and motivational ability that I felt was needed to pull the business out of the doldrums: all businesses need a leader who can make it feel exciting and important. Dudley, their father, said he wanted to hand over the reins but I had my doubts that the boys could cope, which was why, despite his 'retirement', Dudley still felt he had a use. Unfortunately he was part of the problem: his continued and somewhat passive-aggressive presence was hampering progress and sapping his sons' confidence. It was clear that something radical would have to be done: an experienced manager was needed to help put the business back on track – but who? No one within the company seemed to fit the bill. During the course of my investigations I discovered that there had been, some years previously, a manager named Gordon Dick who had been respected and successful, slightly feared on the shop floor but strong on motivation and setting targets. For reasons that were less than well thought through, he had been asked to retire early from the company and that had seemed to mark the beginning of the slide into losses. In the event, I managed to track Gordon down and engineered a meeting between him and the family. Although he harboured some resentment at having been previously ousted from a business he had helped make profitable, as soon as Dudley (unprompted by me, I am pleased to report) suggested he return as chairman, suddenly I felt that the solution to the company's problems was opening up. I saw a future in which Dudley and Tim were free to pursue other interests, while County Linen was brought back to its former glory with Gordon as chairman and Anthony as managing director. With Gordon's guidance, ability and experience Anthony – an able operator, but to my mind quite insecure – might just pull it off. Once again, finding a workable leadership structure would be crucial.

PERSONALITY CHECKLIST

This is an exercise designed to help you to identify how close you are to being a good leader. Bear in mind that, as someone else's assessment of you might be more accurate than your own, it can be useful to find an objective colleague to discuss this with. Use it also as a mental checklist when searching for a new leader for a business or team.

Give yourself a score from 0 to 4 in the space beside each question, where 0 = not the case, 1 = hardly ever the case, 2 = sometimes the case, 3 = often the case , 4 = usually or always the case. Add up your total when you have completed the exercise.

I want to lead others ☐
I give people clear goals ☐
I am a practical person ☐
I can think clearly and logically ☐
I prepare and research thoroughly ☐
I have good gut instincts ☐
I am able to be motivational and inspiring ☐
People come to me for advice ☐
I make decisions reasonably quickly ☐
I am at ease when asking people to do things for me ☐
I am organized ☐
I am good at dealing with stressful situations ☐
I enjoy new challenges ☐
I can see through complicated situations to find solutions ☐
I encourage each person individually ☐
I am seen as someone whom others would wish to follow ☐
I reward good performance ☐
I follow up on what I ask of people ☐
I believe I have people's respect and trust ☐
I am excited by what I am doing ☐

If your total score is in the 0–40 range, your talents probably lie in another direction. It doesn't mean it is impossible for you to run something eventually, but it does mean that you will need to do some serious work on your skills. Don't worry; true leaders are few and far between, while effective team players and back-up staff are essential for successful businesses. Read this book to see what your boss should be doing and where you can help.

If your total score falls between 41 and 65, you are showing potential and need to work on the areas where you have scored the lowest. You may make it to managing director one day, but meanwhile you can make a valuable contribution as a manager. Perhaps you are just starting out, or perhaps you need to take stock and revise some of the ways you are doing things. This book will help you focus on those areas you need to improve.

A total score between 66 and 80 indicates that you do have many of the qualities that make effective leaders. Work through this book carefully to ensure that you are prepared for the challenges that lie ahead.

CHAPTER TWO

▶ Taking charge of the future

The most important thing is to decide what the devil it is that you're trying to do

I explained in the last chapter that one of the essential elements of good leadership is to have a clear vision of where you are taking the company. What this comes down to is having a sensible, workable plan for the next few years. Objectives are essential for success: I know of no one who can make things happen unless these are clearly laid out. Without an aim you will merely be fumbling in the dark. As a leader it is your prime role to work out the direction for the company, so if there is a strategy department get rid of it immediately and do the strategic thinking yourself.

When I look at organizations that are having problems, I usually find that the reason is that they have not thought about the big picture hard enough. This was made abundantly clear in the *I'll Show Them Who's Boss* programmes: I asked each 'candidate' to present their views on what they would do with the company over the next five years should they find themselves in charge. This threw most of them into turmoil – few of them had given this any thought, understandably perhaps in some cases. What then happened was very interesting: my request forced the individuals concerned to look at the issues that were facing their business in a systematic way and drew out some genuinely good ideas (usually accompanied by a good deal of waffle). There was only one presentation, however, that gave me what I was looking for – and I was so impressed that I am including it in its entirety (see page 56).

First things first: assess your current position

I know I haven't made any money
for several years, and I don't know
exactly why. Something is there staring
me in the face and I can't see it for some reason
ROBIN HARRIS, Arrow Ford

It is dangerously easy to formulate grandiose strategic plans that stand no chance of working in reality. It can be great fun to do this, of course, but it is harmful. Don't be tempted by what you would like to do, and for goodness' sake don't do anything until you have collected some very hard information. Only then can you start to think about moving the company forward.

We've never had to do something like
that before. It was the kick we needed
GEORGE CLARK, The Old Manor Hotel

Take a long, hard, ruthlessly honest look at exactly what you have got *now*. Examine and map out every single aspect of your business, so that you end up with a logical, clear analysis of where you stand. Look at what is working, what is not working, who is good, what machinery and other assets you have, what the reputation of the business is, how each department is performing. You need to know sales figures and profitability for the past three years. All the problems, all the pitfalls: the good, the bad and the ugly. What you will end up with is a mixture of solid financial facts and calm analysis that indicates what will happen *if you do nothing*. This kind of 'baseline thinking' is, in my view, rarely done properly.

We are not running out of ideas
but we are running out of time
ANTHONY MOORE, County Linen

Collecting this information is not as difficult as it may sound, but it is time-consuming, so give yourself a couple of months if you are new in the job or if it has not been done for some time. Be as wide-ranging in your data-gathering as possible, assign others to certain research projects if necessary, and don't forget to:

Talk to your customers

This is an incredibly useful exercise to go through in order to find out what people really think of your products or services. Ask them which of your competitors they use, what they like and dislike about your company, how they think the market is moving. Put yourself in their shoes – try to think like a customer.

Join trade associations if you are new to the industry

You will begin to network informally with people in the same industry as yourself, which is useful for knowing who you are up against and for gaining a sense of what is going on in general. It will also help you to be aware of market trends and new legislation that might affect your business sector. (A word of warning: when you already are part of an industry you can waste a lot of time with these associations, so don't get too sucked in.)

Avoid industry 'experts' like the plague

Only talk to those who know by having done it.

Watch your competitors like a hawk

Find out as much as possible without resorting to industrial espionage. I am a huge believer in copying success, because hardly anything you set out to do hasn't been done before. Use your competitors' products, go to their shops or showrooms, visit their sites. It may even be possible to talk frankly to some of the chief executives, particularly those outside your geographical area: they should be flattered by your approach and may offer a wealth of useful information.

Talk to your staff

All strategic plans end in something physical having to be done by people at the sharp end, and these people are acutely aware of what bothers them. Ask them how they do things, what could be done better, and whether they have

any ideas for new initiatives that would dramatically improve their own job –
but only ask them questions to which they will know the answers.

The day Henry walks through these
gates involved in the fruit is the
day I shall leave
MANAGER OF FRUIT FARM, Norwood Park

Things do need to change:
staff, work, everything
WORKER, County Linen

Brainstorm for ideas among the tier of managers who report to you
This is particularly useful, as these are the people who are going to have to
help carry out the strategy when it is finalized, and you need their 'buy-in'.

Look at your internal processes
Think about the levels of bureaucracy, the forms that get filled in before
something can happen. Look at the meetings that go on, the company
structure, the reporting lines ... anything that hampers speed and efficiency.
It has been my own experience that most bureaucracy is not only
unnecessary but positively harmful. People who couldn't plan their way out
of a paper bag love paperwork.

Consider outside factors that might affect your business
These might be such things as a new train station bringing new customers;
a rival opening an office nearby; a big plant shutting down nearby; or interest
rates and how they affect bank borrowing. Beware of making decisions based
on larger trends - it is notoriously difficult to make sensible business decisions
based on global-economy forecasts. Stick to what is real and obvious.

I've done more thinking in the
last week than I have in the
past four years
SIMON, George Brown & Sons

Stop! Don't be a swot

What all too many managers will do at this point is draw up a pretty SWOT chart: a boxed grid listing the company's strengths, weaknesses, opportunities and threats. They will be very proud of it; they may even show it to a few people. Then they will put it away and forget about it. I hate formalized documents like this – they leach creativity and remove responsibility, and they are a total waste of time. What my system does is get you to do the SWOT-type thinking and then move straight on to action. I was pleased to see that some of the individuals in *I'll Show Them Who's Boss* had started to think along these lines, although none of them went far enough.

What a leader really needs to end up with from the above exercise is an awareness of the following:

- What makes your company special
- Which areas you need to improve
- Where potential problems lie
- What the financial picture looks like

and above all:

- Where the opportunities for expansion lie, and how you are going to reach new customers, develop new products and enter new markets.

Improving what you do and increasing profitability is ultimately what your strategy should be all about. Your purpose as a leader is to develop a plan that leads you towards this end.

Devising a strategic plan

If he doesn't know what he's doing
or where this company is going, then
how are the rest of us supposed to know?
Jo, Arrow Ford

There are three major elements to your long-term strategy:

1 An Overall Vision

To introduce your strategy you need a one-sentence statement which sums up why you exist, what you are, what your business is, how it differentiates itself from the competition and where you are going. Often called a 'mission statement', it should be simple, clear and straightforward. It will be informed by your sense of vision – how you see the future – and you will believe in it with a passion.

For example, possible mission statements for some of the *I'll Show Them Who's Boss* businesses might be:

Muncaster Castle: To generate sufficient income to maintain the castle in excellent order for future generations, both as a family home and as a building of genuine historic interest.

AMT Espresso: To continue to offer top-quality, good-value coffee at attractive, customer-driven outlets throughout the United Kingdom and Ireland.

The Old Manor Hotel: To maintain The Old Manor Hotel as a highly respected and profitable business, and within five years acquire a pub/restaurant and double the overall profit of the group.

County Linen: Firstly, to get back into profit; and thereafter to build the most profitable and highest quality operator in the UK laundry business.

Arrow Ford: To become the biggest, most highly regarded and most profitable Ford dealership in Wales over the next ten years.

2 The Strategic Overview

*This process has set the cat among
the pigeons but it's woken everyone*

up ... all these brainwaves are
appearing from nowhere
SIMON, George Brown & Sons

This should be no more than a few pages long, with details relevant to the readers. You will need to include the following:

- an overview of the business/es with relevant historical information
- salient facts about the current situation (what you are selling, how and to whom)
- the financial performance over the past three years
- the forecast for the next year
- financial projections for the following 3–5 years
- key issues facing the business
- objectives (which will usually be to do what you are doing, but to do it better and more efficiently)
- a brief outline of your strategies for meeting these objectives

There are two important things to remember here. Don't get bogged down in complex details, and don't be frightened: you don't necessarily need to be formulating something grand and amazing. Sometimes it is worth saying, 'We do what we do well and we're going to carry on doing it'. Make the overview clear, direct and to the point. (At the end of this chapter you will find as an example the review I wrote as the new chief executive of Granada back in 1991, when my objective for the first year was just to survive!) Your objectives should be stretching, but possible; you must be able to measure progress towards them (for example, in terms of sales or customer satisfaction levels), and of course they must lead the business towards greater profits.

It is helpful when preparing this to go back to those people who helped in the initial brainstorming. Encourage them to feel that some of the ideas are their own, or that at the least they have contributed to setting the company's objectives. In the end it is immaterial who claims ideas as their own; the important thing is to have your people on board, particularly as new strategies nearly always involve a process of change – and change is tough to manage at the best of times.

An obvious point, but one that is often missed – keep this document to hand, refer to it often, and use it as your starting-point when you come to plan next year's objectives.

3 The Action Plan

We discuss things, I will suggest
things, but we're just not doing anything
SAM, Arrow Ford

Now to the specifics. No amount of strategic thinking is worth the paper it is written on unless you make it happen, which is why planning is the most important aspect of taking charge of your company's future. Take the key issues, objectives and broad-brush strategies from your overview, and break them down into hard action points. This means giving:

- detailed and specific tasks which need to be performed – step by step, by whom, and by when (month by month)
- month-by-month sales forecasts and profit and loss figures

For example, if Arrow Ford needed to open a new car showroom by the end of the next year in order to meet financial targets, there is a critical path that needs to be followed in order to complete this objective on time. When I was at Granada we wanted to bring in new products at the Little Chef restaurants. Before these could be introduced, in some outlets microwaves were needed, in some extra power, in some both – so we had to draw up a plan for installing these before we could move to the next step of the new product launch. We also wanted new uniforms, so we had to get these designed, approved, manufactured, distributed – and so on. Everything in your big picture is affected by many hundreds of smaller tasks carried out by the tiers of people further down the organization. Everyone has their part to play in taking the company towards your vision, so you must leave nothing to chance. I will talk about how to communicate your strategy to your staff in a later chapter.

To ensure that this action plan becomes the ultimate useful document, keep in mind my watchwords:

Clarity
Simplicity
Follow-up

and as you tick off the completed action points month by month at the meetings with your subordinates (see page 22), you will see your vision and objectives become reality.

Reviewing your strategy, refining your vision

There's more to be done than I realized
ANTHONY MOORE, County Linen

While this method is as foolproof as any I know, it does not guarantee that the unexpected will not happen. Your action plan is a rolling document that will need to be adjusted every so often to accommodate the hiccups that will no doubt occur. Products go out of date, new trends and fashions emerge, new competitors enter the market, new restrictions are brought in, there are inevitable delays and setbacks. Equally, however, a change to your strategy might be brought on by something more exciting. I often think that strategy documents can limit a leader's thinking. Sometimes you need to be able to respond quickly to a change in market conditions or a new business opportunity – and fill in the details afterwards. Take the orders, then go back and organize the machinery to fulfil them. It is often better, after all, to have the customers first than spend a fortune on preparing to serve a new market before you are certain it is there.

The most important thing is to be consistent with your strategy and never to change your mind about the fundamental direction the company is going in. But (and it's a big 'but') at the same time you must be willing to stop if the strategy is genuinely failing. How do you know? Well, that is your call as leader, and only you will recognize the indications. By keeping a watchful eye on the action plan with its financial targets, you will see clearly when reality is so far removed from your plan that it is time to cut your losses and move on.

While strategic planning is your job as leader, you should also try to develop a vibrant culture of alertness, fact-finding and innovation among your staff, so that the company is pulling together towards the common goal of producing fine products that people want, in an efficient and profitable way.

Strategic vision was very obviously lacking in the businesses we filmed. In order to help people define where they wanted to take the business, I asked various individuals to present their strategic plans to me. It was a useful exercise for me to see who had the best grasp of business basics, where the passion and vision lay, and who might be the potential new leaders.

*   *   *

Each brother at **AMT Espresso** talked about having a mission, and broadly they had the same objective: to be the leading brand of top-quality, value-for-money coffee with the best customer service. Angus was a little incoherent, but he wanted to improve consistency across the different outlets, expand into new markets and tighten the company's internal workings. Alastair's presentation was full of passion and bombast, and idea upon idea poured out of him. He saw the need for staff incentives, better marketing and packaging, proactive planning, and a more controlled meetings system. But in his presentation to me he failed to show that he had a firm grasp of the figures and, as I recall, gave me his financial goals without being certain what was realistic in terms of expansion. Allan was short and sweet with his presentation (which always pleases me). He was very clear on what he did not think the company should do in terms of joint ventures, acquisitions and new markets. He simply stated that in order to maintain its position as well-priced, nicely fitted-out, well-located coffee bars, it needed to have around a hundred bars by the end of the next five years. He even supported his projections with figures, and showed how he could use the people who were already in the business – strong, solid stuff. It was a good, straightforward strategy, if a bit unadventurous, and I was impressed with his clarity of thought.

None of the brothers' presentations gave me a five-year strategy, and to be honest I hadn't expected any of them to. Only a few days before, after all, they had been fretting about a gas cylinder on a trolley, so to expect them to be clear about the way to take the business forward was probably asking too much. It's a very difficult task, but one I had to set them, and for me it certainly pointed to the one obvious leader.

*   *   *

George Brown & Sons had been in business for 115 years. Sales and profits were falling due to an increasingly competitive market-place and lack of leadership. When I first asked the family what their objective was, I was told it was 'to earn a living for all of us and pay our way and keep going'. They soon realized this was not enough.

I was interested to hear how the individuals concerned might see the future of the business. What emerged was a clear split between those who were reliable, efficient team members, good at their jobs, but who couldn't see beyond their own particular patch; and those who had ambitions to lead and had thought about the broader issues. Those with the ideas were the younger generation: Lorraine, Phillip and Simon. They all recognized that there was a need to separate the sales and delivery functions (and hence to increase sales and reduce the cost of deliveries), to bring in computerized invoicing and stock control, to improve customer relations, to seek out new customers in the hotel, pub and convenience-store sectors, to expand geographically and beef up marketing. Lorraine was keen on launching a website and branching out into a fruit version of Interflora, and even talked of doing packaging for other companies. Phillip was keen on sorting out the mechanics of the delivery process and maximizing sales to existing customers. All mentioned the pre-packed market, while some talked of moving into exotic produce, meat and cheese – and even flowers, chips and Christmas trees. Jim told me about the changing nature of the market and different buying habits, and worried that no one followed up on lost customers. Paul was concerned to tighten up on wasted time and money. No one presented any hard figures or research, and I was concerned that some of these ideas might take them away from their core business.

Lorraine had a good financial sense and was already doing a good job as company administrator; she was methodical and well liked, although she tended to put herself down. Phillip had a good organizational sense but I felt he would find it hard to lift his eyes above the operational level. David admitted that he was bereft of ideas and, more important from a leadership standpoint, I felt he lacked any drive for taking the business forward, although he clearly enjoyed his purchasing role.

It was Simon's presentation, however, that stood out a mile. He had thought about a 'mission', which was to 'be the premier supplier of fresh produce to the retail and catering sections in the South West'. He had prepared a sensible analysis of where the company was at and where he saw it going. He selected a few key areas for sales-growth potential. He had drawn up a structure for the company and had ideas for sorting out roles and job descriptions, seemed to understand about targeting and about motivating the sales force, and knew exactly which individuals were good at what. He made me feel that the move into 'pre-pack' was a real goer for the company under his management. He was even aware of the need to manage change. Not only was he temperamentally suited to lead, he also had a decent plan. It had to be him.

* * *

I didn't need to ask Iona of **Muncaster Castle** for a presentation to prove that she would be the best leader. I could see that she was bursting with ideas and just needed to be given the chance to get on with them. I did sit down with her and thrash out some specific medium- and long-term plans, and this is a condensed version of how it looked.

MUNCASTER CASTLE STRATEGIC OVERVIEW

Objective

To produce a certain revenue by the year 2010 in order to enable the castle to be maintained in excellent order for future generations. This end to be achieved without the loss of Muncaster as a family home and without losing the integrity of the castle as a building of genuine historic interest.

The plan looked at sources of income and how these might be further exploited.

Property

The castle itself

Some visitors already stay overnight, usually attracted by the castle's rumoured ghosts. This 'haunted house' aspect could be exploited further. There are also other sections of the castle which could be converted into luxury rooms for letting.

Accommodation block
This could be exploited further, with more rooms, higher occupancy rates and higher prices.

The Pennington Arms
A derelict hotel already being converted into holiday accommodation, with possibilities for a restaurant.

The dairy
Currently derelict, but with potential for conversion to bridal suite.

Owned houses
More potential for income generation.

Entrance fees
Examine relationship between price and volume of visitors. Add to demand for entrance and increase entrance price.

Weddings and events
Muncaster is a popular venue, so it is feasible to aim for fewer events at higher net return. Explore other events such as golf, fishing, shooting, painting, music and cookery.

Catering
Potentially highly profitable but is currently underexploited.

Retail
Currently underexploited.

Other attractions
These are currently the maze and the owlery. Consider testing separate entrance prices.

Off-site sales

Huge opportunities for marketing the castle itself via the website, plus promoting sales of, for example, toys, books and plants.

Grants and sponsorship

Some progress has already been made on winning grants for castle repairs. Explore the possibility of employing a student or retired person to look into other funding opportunities, such as a 'Friends of Muncaster' scheme.

A separate schedule to the strategy document gave detailed plans for each of these areas. For example, in order to improve the gardens the tasks to be actioned included:

- recruit new gardener
- improve labelling and plant 'story-telling'
- connect plant stories to plants available for purchase
- plan marketing of Roman ruins
- relaunch gardens around the story of the ruins and run PR campaign

Under each of these headings was a step-by-step list of tasks to be completed, by whom and by when.

I was absolutely amazed by the professionalism of the presentation made to me by George and Michael Clark at **The Old Manor Hotel**, Fife. Once they were given the chance to produce some solid plans they came up trumps. It was so good that I will include it here.

THE OLD MANOR HOTEL – STRATEGIC OVERVIEW

Background
- Family business started in 1992 by the Clark family
- Limited company – all shares owned by principals
- Father and two sons
- Currently operating one hotel unit purchased out of receivership
- Current site (The Old Manor Hotel) has been developed over eleven years by investing profits in expanding businesses, e.g.:

Developments at TOMH
- Run-down pub transformed into busy successful pub/bistro
- Function suite extended and modernized to create new business opportunities
- Additional bedrooms
- Purchase of adjacent property to offer additional/alternative accommodation
- Creation of new restaurant concept and improvement of visual aspect by creation of a new atrium foyer

Current position
- Market research/bench-marking shows that the hotel is well managed, profitable and well above average in terms of average room rate, room occupancy
- This has been achieved through tough trading conditions in an unfashionable location
- Market value of business in current conditions is around 7–8 times original purchase price. At this value gearing is about 20-25 per cent

Crossroads
- Major shareholder is at retirement age
- In view of previous information, bank is begging to lend more money for succession/expansion
- Further expansion on site would be capital investment with a slow return on investment
- While organic growth by developing the existing business is possible, it is considered that this would not be at the rate of previous years

Options
1 Sell to willing buyers at a good price with a healthy return on investment
2 Leave alone as it is running very nicely – continue with organic growth
3 Take advantage of low interest rates/gearing to buy out major shareholder now
4 Take advantage of low gearing and gear up to expand

Decisions and reasons
1 Sell

Doesn't actually make much sense to do this, as the hotel is still a cash cow and can assist better as a going concern to finance new ventures until they become self-financing. We don't think we would be satisfied with selling ultimately, and it would certainly lead to missed opportunities.

2 Do Nothing

Tempting to do nothing, but we are at our best when grappling with the challenge of development and expansion.

3 Buy-out

AC doesn't want to retire at present unless we want him to. Our view is that if he is willing to help we would like to explore the opportunities for expansion with his expertise on board.

A consideration is that under the present investment climate he would only attain the same return from another business venture. We would rather have him in partnership with us as he wants to continue working anyway.

4 Expand
By elimination this is our preferred option.

Investment opportunities on site

- Land development into studios
  Long-term project, probably a slow return on investment. Might be better left with planning consent as a carrot for a potential investor.
- Leisure centre
  Heavy investment – dubious return for a property of this size in an area with a relatively small indigenous population.
- Ongoing refurbishment and improvement of existing facilities
  We would pursue this option in any case to improve income and protect/enhance the valuation.

External investment

1 Type of property – hotel/restaurant/pub
Our preference is for a pub/restaurant. We have the template for doing this in the Coachman's [a pub attached to the front of The Old Manor Hotel] which has been our biggest success to date, and for a small capital outlay. Our target business is something which has been run down, neglected, or is not operating to its full potential.

We are not looking for a hotel because:
- We have looked at a few locally and some further afield. None seem to offer the same potential as The Old Manor Hotel (TOMH) when we first saw it. At the moment there is too high a premium on the property value rather than the return on capital.
- A hotel in a location too close to TOMH would leave us doubly

vulnerable to a continuation of the tourist downturn and could also potentially dilute the restaurant business we already have. We may need to dilute our staff establishment in an area where we know recruitment is already difficult.

2 How many?

One to start with to see how the template works. If we can do this, who knows how many will follow?

3 Location

Our target area would be in the suburbs or a larger conurbation. We are not looking for a city centre location as we believe the Coachman's concept would not work as well there. Entry cost (freehold or leasehold) would be more reasonable, and as more businesses and retail outlets are locating out of town there is more potential there.

4 Stage in the product cycle of existing business to be bought over

We are not looking to buy into a mature business which will have an established customer base and will attract a premium price. Our target business will be like TOMH was, a previously successful business in a target location which has fallen on hard times through poor management. A business with growth potential which needs regeneration of the product and its mix.

5 Outright purchase of freehold or alternatively a leasehold

Twelve years ago when we were looking to purchase TOMH we were scared off leaseholds because of the market conditions then prevailing. Now there may be advantages to leaseholds without the same pitfalls. A long leasehold may enhance our potential to expand/develop further or sell on.

- Consequences/Opportunities for existing business

We will seek to recruit locally for key staff in the area of our new venture. We will not initially use our existing staff on the new site. Management will be spread more thinly in the initial stages, as we seek to develop our new venture, so the opportunities for advancement at TOMH may well result.

In some key areas, e.g. purchasing, accounting and payroll, we will be able to use our existing systems to achieve savings in overhead.
We will cross-sell the new venture through our Loyalty Club and offer deals at The Old Manor for customers at our new venture. We believe that after eleven years of growth and quality recognition, we have the personnel with a track record to maintain the business continuity.

- The next steps
We have identified two pubs on the outskirts of Edinburgh which conform to our product-cycle analysis and location preference. Currently both businesses are brewery owned (different breweries). Both operate as managed houses, and both have a food operation which scratches the surface of their potential. Neither is presently on the market. We have asked our property agents to establish contact with the operators to establish if they might look to sale or lease.

I was impressed with this presentation because:
- It is an excellent analysis of the past and the now
- It looks at a sensible list of alternative strategies
- It 'makes a decision' on what to do
- It can now be used to plan the way forward in a series of measurable tasks

Interestingly, the DO IT part was where the brothers fell down: they baulked at getting it under way. To find out what happened next, see page 144.

* * *

Robin at **Arrow Ford** had not got to first base on devising a strategy. He wasn't even on top of how the business was doing compared with the last month, or the last year. There was no monthly review system, and no financial information made available to each department. I was astonished that the company had kept going for so long under these constraints. On the other hand, Nigel Bond at 'Rapid Fit' was very clear on how he made his money: 'Speak to the people, get into the companies, give them a service at the end of the day. Someone turns up – make them feel special and get it sorted for them.' And his objective? 'I've got a thousand customers, and if I can keep a thousand customers happy that will do me fine.'

Before they could even start to formulate a strategy, I asked Robin and Nigel to start dealing with the numbers in a serious way: to use the previous year's figures as a budget for the current year, and to produce a monthly profit and loss account. I also asked the two of them to involve Robin's daughters in formulating an outline of a plan for the next few years. I was sure there was potential for the company, not least because Phil the accountant had said that if they had 1 per cent of the amount of business in the area, they would be bursting at the seams. Now that Nigel is in charge, I expect to see him overhauling all the systems and business processes, improving communication throughout the company, focusing on sales, marketing and customer care, and providing monthly targets for each area of the business. Once this has been achieved, he may want to look at strategic issues such as whether the Ford franchise is the best way forward, whether the body-shop side of the business should be expanded, and whether to continue with 'Rapid Fit'. Whatever direction he takes it in, it is certain that when Sam and Jo eventually inherit their father's 51 per cent it will be a business worth having.

* * *

The three businesses at **Norwood Park** had muddled along for years, and each one had the potential to be far more profitable. This had become a stark necessity, as the house was in danger of falling into disrepair and I believed that the current income (around £50k from golf; £75k from the fruit and £25k from events) was not enough to provide a salary for Sir John and Lady Starkey, running costs for the house and sufficient cash to renovate it on an ongoing basis. It was astonishing to me that no one was clear about the, say, ten most important things that needed to be done in the next year to keep the show on the road. So I asked the three contenders from among the children (Henry and Georgie, Suzannah and Johnno, and Elizabeth and Alex) to go away and formulate their own strategies for Norwood Park – how they would improve the existing businesses and find extra long-term income. What emerged was very interesting. Henry gave a characteristically vague and muddled presentation under the title of Norwood Park, Inc. Elizabeth had some well-thought-through ideas for converting the house into a 'hip hotel'. Suzannah and Johnno had a cogent plan for transforming the house into a high-spec family home with top facilities that could be opened up to high-paying delegates for a house-party-style business. I was left in no doubt that Suzannah and Johnno's bid was the strongest, and that they were capable and willing to take on the management of Norwood Park. In reality, the business solutions were relatively simple. The most important strategic decision was who was to be in charge. Sir John Starkey had his own views, and although I strongly recommended he choose Suzannah as the right person for the job I knew he was so guided by tradition that in his eyes Henry was the only choice.

* * *

A laundry business can be really difficult because it runs on tight margins. You need to get the quality absolutely right: stained, lost and damaged linen will not endear you to your customers. Your staff, who are often on the minimum wage, need to be motivated to produce quality work, quickly. Your machinery needs to be working to capacity, and you need good sales and marketing people drumming up new business. In short, the problem facing **County Linen** was how to get more laundry washed more quickly and in top condition, with the same number of employees; or, in their terms, more pieces per operator hour (PPOH). As a first step towards finding out what was going on, Tim and Anthony Moore were asked to go on to the shop floors of both plants to talk to their staff. This was one of those exercises that managers hate doing: it's hard to hear home truths, yet it is absolutely crucial in the path towards understanding how to fix a troubled business. Good managers need to be able to take a certain amount of stick and the two men were assailed by all manner of complaints. This should have marked the start of a period of some weeks in which the brothers applied themselves to asking detailed questions of individuals, and to looking long and hard at what was working well and what was not. There were big questions in my mind to do with reporting structures, quality control, complaints procedures, discipline, motivation, modernization and – obviously – leadership. It was a great chance to crunch some numbers and analyse various possible solutions, and then to involve me in deciding how to move forward. Sadly, as often happens in this situation, the brothers found this period of learning just too difficult to keep going with. Anthony cut the process short and rushed into announcing a bonus scheme that was not fully thought through. I suppose he hoped it would jump-start productivity, and improve morale and his popularity. The announcement was reasonably well received but, because it didn't deliver to employees very quickly, it fell flat and productivity flatlined. What a wasted opportunity.

* * *

One of my first tasks on arrival at the troubled Granada empire was to formulate a strategy for turning around the business. It took me about eight weeks to research and write, and when implemented had the desired effect. It is probably not a perfect template for a strategic plan, and you should not read it as such. I merely include it here as a real-life example of something that worked.

STRICTLY PRIVATE & CONFIDENTIAL

GRANADA GROUP PLC
SHORT TO MEDIUM TERM REVIEW

BY G J ROBINSON
29.11.91

GRANADA GROUP PLC
I have now completed an outline review of the main elements in Granada Group PLC and have had a chance to meet most of the senior management teams. In addition, we have carried out a first round of monthly detailed operational reviews on the performance of period 1 for each of the main divisions.

It is worth perhaps clarifying that I see my own initial task as one of settling the Group down to concentrating on running the main businesses that we now have (there are still a number of small potential disposals) in a much tighter and more profit/cost conscious way. This will inevitably involve a rather more hands-on approach than has been the case in the past which may, at least initially, lead to some discomfort in some areas.

The make-up of the Group is as follows:
1 UK TV Rental (including Granada Business Communications)
2 Granada Television
3 Leisure – including
>   Motorways
>   Bowling
>   Nightclubs
>   Theme Parks
>   Travel
>   Other (Lakewoods, USA Bingo, Interactive Video)
4 Computer Services
5 International (including Kapy)
6 Head Office

I outline below what I see as the key elements for each of these constituent parts of the Group.

1. UK TV RENTAL
I believe that we have an excellent business here which is capable of giving strong profits and cash flows long into the future. It is certainly true that it is likely, in the long run, to be in slow decline as prices for new televisions, video recorders and satellite installations fall in real terms and as their reliability improves. This makes the purchase option an easier one for the customer. Our management task, therefore, falls into four distinct parts:

>   1 Keep the decline in installation as low as possible and/or
>   halt/reverse it should the opportunity present itself
>   2 Improve the pricing for greater margin at the same time as
>   we reduce the capital spend
>   3 Gain an increasing share of the retail market but only where
>   it is clearly profitable to do so
>   4 Reduce costs vigorously

The profit history of the business (excluding GBC) has been as follows:

£m	1988/89	1989/90		1990/91		Budget 1991/92	
			%		%		%
Gross Income	316	329	+4	341	+4	356	+4
Depreciation	(74)	(65)	-12	(70)	+8	(75)	+7
Costs	(151)	(190)	+26	(197)	+4	(207)	+5
PBIT	91	74	-19	74		74	

This is a trend that, although a creditable performance, particularly against our major competitors, were it to continue in real terms would unacceptably reduce the value of the business over the next ten years. I have agreed with the divisional management that we should seek, through a combination of intelligent price increases and vigorous cost cutting, to reverse the trend. For example, an effective 2.5% price increase combined with a 5% cost reduction would move the 1991/2 PBIT to £99m compared to the £74m budgeted. These are not huge shifts and although undoubtedly painful are well within the boundaries of sensible targeting. This exercise is now being studied and plans for its execution should be available to be put into effect early in the new year. I do not anticipate that we will achieve the full £99m in the financial year for timing reasons, but we should take a worthwhile step along the way.

Strategically I believe that we should continue to buy small 'add-on' rental businesses as the opportunities present themselves, we should fully integrate the business rental side into the mainstream business and we should consider moving the non-TV/Video maintenance operation into the Computer Services division. I believe that the decision not to go into white goods rental is the right one. There is clearly considerable scope for profit growth in the next two to three years as we take the opportunity to reduce operating costs and to price upwards in a steady and intelligently controlled way. There may also be longer term opportunities to rationalize the shop network but this needs careful handling.

2. GRANADA TELEVISION

The recent award of the franchise at what is clearly an excellent price is a wonderful starting point for the future of this business. All other things being equal we should manage to hold on to the franchise for the next twenty years. The TV operation as it now stands is made up of three separate, albeit inter-relating parts:

Broadcasting
Production & Distribution
The Studios Tour (and the Victoria & Albert Hotel)

Following the franchise debacle, there is little doubt, perhaps sadly, that the old, more comfortable, era of ever increasing advertising revenues, of selling at fixed prices to the network, of sharing often rapidly increasing network costs and of having a virtual monopoly within which to operate is over. The high prices paid for their franchises by a number of operators, together with the emergence of new operators, particularly Carlton in London, will change the face and pace of the industry. Increasingly too, the appearance of satellite in more and more homes will begin to eat into the monopoly advertising position. Tightly controlled budgets, particularly on the production side, with an increase in the use of independent producers for new material will be the order of the day. Granada Television has a proud history of being a quality player as a producer/broadcaster, and its reputation and standing were undoubtedly key factors in winning its franchise on such favourable terms. Ironically, in the new scenario, that tradition may make it more difficult to adapt to the new commercial reality.

The profit history is as follows:

£m	Actual 1988/89	Actual 1989/90	%	Actual 1990/91	%	Budget 1991/92	%
Total Income	252	250	-1	254	+2	257	+1
Granada Costs	(115)	(110)	-4	(120)	+9	(121)	+1
Industry/ network costs	(89)	(91)	+2	(102)	+12	(106)	+4
Profit before levy	48	49	+4	32	-35	30	-6
Levy	(16)	(17)		(12)		(14)*	
PBIT	32	32		20		16	

* Excludes recent levy change.

Here again is a downward trend that clearly cannot be allowed to continue. There is little doubt that pressure on advertising income will continue as long as the recession does, and it is too early to know what kind of programme pricing structure will emerge among the franchise holders. Together with the rest of the industry, we increased our programme expenditure in the run-up to the new franchise awards. We should, of course, adhere to any agreements with the ITC, but it is clear that we need now to tackle our own cost base firmly and to contribute where we can to achieving an overall cost reduction in the network schedule costs. As examples, a 20% cost reduction in our own costs and a standstill on industry costs would produce a profit before levy of £54m in 91/92, a 10% own cost reduction and similar standstill in industry costs would produce £43m. I believe that our cost base is high and that something of the order of a 20% real reduction is achievable given the will to do so. As might be anticipated there are conflicting views on this. The debate has begun – but, clearly, we must get past that stage quickly if we are to make a worthwhile impact on this year's numbers.

Strategically I believe that we have a powerful profit and cash producer in this division and that that is not at all inconsistent with our wish to be the highest quality operator in the network. If we are able to produce good returns from the business, we will be in a strong position in the medium term to acquire other operators, particularly locally, where combining them will give opportunities for cost rationalisation – a process that will almost certainly go on with or without us. We have a huge site in Manchester that, on balance, is something of a liability because it is far in excess of our needs and is expensive to operate. With the present state of the property market and our own shortage of funds it would be foolish to try to solve that problem now, but it is probable that over the coming years a new, much smaller facility would make sense. In the meantime we have developed a mini theme park (Studios Tour) on the site and we are in the process of building a hotel (the Victoria & Albert). So far, despite a better than expected volume of visitors, the theme park loses money after interest and I am personally doubtful about the commercial viability of the hotel.

Our short term aim should be to try to make a sensible return on our investment in the Studios Tour before we commit ourselves to further developments, and to review thoroughly our options on the hotel.

3. LEISURE

We have a number of separate businesses of various sizes in this division. The key one is our *motorway services operation*, albeit that in some ways it is in fact two separate businesses, motorway service areas 'proper' and trunk road sites. It is no surprise that the motorway operations are relatively successful but the trunk road sites show very poor returns. The motorway operation is a sound business and, if average returns can be improved, it has good potential for steady long-term profits. The future of the trunk road sites and associated hotels is doubtful. The profit history is as follows:

£m	1989/90	1990/91	Budget 1991/92
Income	218	240	256
Cost of Sales	(181)	(200)	(213)
Gross Profit	37	40	43
Costs	(21)	(23)	(26)
PBIT	16	17	17
Interest	(5)	(9)	(8)
PBT	11	8	9
Av. Capital Emp'd	155	164	182
Return on ROCE	10.3%	10.4%	9.3%
ROCE: On Original Cost	15.5%	15.2%	13.1%

The picture here is of steadily increasing investment against static profits, again a picture that cannot be allowed to continue. We have recently recruited Charles Allen, previously MD of Compass Catering, to head up the Leisure division and his first task will be to conduct a thorough review of the motorway operation with a view to significant margin improvement. Again as an example some quite small improvements in margin (+0.25% forecourt, +2.5% catering, +2% shops and +5% lodges) together with modest overhead reduction would produce a PBIT of £23.1m, a PBT of £14.9m and a return on average capital employed of 12.7% which, although still unacceptable, would be beginning to look respectable.

Strategically we need to enhance greatly the returns we make from this business (20%+) before we commit further serious investment to it. We will probably need to spend a little more capital on bringing some of the existing locations up to scratch. We need to look at our options on the hotel front, although it is probable that we will seek to dispose of them in due course.

In Ten Pin Bowling, we are the largest operator in the UK with twenty-one sites up and running and a further three under construction. We currently have capital of £40m invested and this is expected to rise to £42.5m by the end of financial year 1992. Although there are obviously some grave doubts about the cyclical nature (faddiness?) of this business against the substantial investment in it, I honestly don't believe that we have seriously made the most of it. I am deeply unimpressed by the senior management here, and as an example of that we had recently eight sites without a general manager – a sorry state of affairs. I believe that we need to make some management changes and generally sharpen up our act before we give any further serious thought to our strategic options.

The picture in *Nightclubs* looks similar. We have ten clubs and five feeder bars with an overall capital investment of £15m. We are currently without a general manager for the operation, and in a business that needs controlling tightly, that is an unhappy situation. The strategy here too must be to run what we have well and consistently before we even begin to decide what our longer term plans might be.

As at the end of last year we had some £43m invested in *Theme Parks* that yielded a 1.4% return on our investment, despite some enthusiastic work on improving attendances. There seems little doubt that our purchases in this area were a mistake and, although we may have to run them for some time to improve their selling profile, we should almost certainly seek to extricate ourselves from this area as soon as it is practicable.

In *Travel*, following earlier disposals, we are left with a collection of three businesses, Air Travel Group (ATG), which organises air travel holidays mainly to Italy, Budget Travel, which operates holidays from Ireland, and Discovery Cruises. With the exception of Budget, which looks like a sound little business, the others produce small losses or minimum profits, huge accounting and administrative headaches and high ongoing risks. We should get out of the lot at the earliest sensible opportunity.

4 COMPUTER SERVICES

Although this has been nothing short of a disaster for the Group, it is a delight to see the extent of the turnaround under John Curran's management. John's style is direct and, in a remarkably short time, he has imposed order on a business that was falling apart. It looks as though we have achieved a worthwhile profit in period 1, and John and his team are confident that that should continue for the rest of the year. That being so, we can take a breathing space to examine the longer term outlook for the business. The key to that will be our ability to reduce the high level of non-renewal on maintenance contracts and to maintain/improve both the level and the quality of new gains. Alongside that issue is the one of establishing a 'permanently employed' management team for the longer term. Within the division, GIS, the in-house programming and processing service needs to be examined as to its suitability to meet our longer term needs.

5 INTERNATIONAL

There are four businesses that rightly belong in this 'division':

Business	Market	Capital employed
US Hospitals	Short-term rental of TVs to hospital patients	30
Canadian Hospitals		6
Telerent (Germany)	TV/Video rental to homes	19
Kapy (Spain)	Electrical goods retail	12
		£67m

All of these businesses are for sale in either the short or medium term. The two North American businesses are currently 'off the market' and John Curran and John O'Brien (to whom they currently report) have been asked to liaise on the short term plans for them. I expect to have a clearer view by the end of the calendar year. Telerent in Germany is effectively to be run down and then the 'rump' is to be sold off. I have yet to decide whether it should report to John Curran, Tom Cole, or another after John O'Brien's departure in April 1992. The sale of Kapy is currently being negotiated, sadly with only one potential purchaser. The price looks dismal, as indeed does the prospect of continuing to run it. If necessary it will report to Charles Allen until we dispose of it.

6. HEAD OFFICE
We are well on the way towards completing a major cost reduction programme for the head office. The revised ongoing annual central costs are now £5m compared to £6.5m originally, a reduction of 23%. The longer term role of head office is to provide only those central services that are unavoidable and to manage the operating companies entirely through the directly reporting divisional managers. That being so we will be seeking every opportunity to reduce costs further in the future.

Summary
It is of course early days, but I believe that the way forward in most areas is clear. With all the risks that it entails I believe that our aim or target in profit terms for 1991/2 should be as follows:

£m PBIT	Latest Budget	'Internal Annual-ised Target'	Sensible Guess
UK Rental	82	99	90
Television	25*	46	30*
Leisure	25	32	29
Computer			
Services	9	9	9
International	1	1	1
Head Office net	(10)	(9)	(5)
Pensions Credit	13	13	13
Total PBIT	145	191	167
Interest	(40)	(35)	(36)
	105	156	131

* includes a £6m reduction in Levy already achieved.

We will certainly give it a good try.

Finally, on cash flow we were looking at a budgeted outflow of £105m. This has already been forecast to reduce to an £81m outflow and I hope that we can reduce that to below £50m. We will begin an exercise shortly to examine what options we have on this front.

CHAPTER THREE

Your people

If you haven't got the staff behind you
... you've already lost

We have looked at the qualities that make a leader, and we have looked at how to work out your plans for the future, but these alone are not enough to ensure long-term success. Of course you need to know what you are doing and where you are going, but to get there you must surround yourself with excellent people in jobs that are right for them. You also need to ensure that they are comfortable in their roles and happy with what is expected of them. If you have good people reporting to you, people who feel part of a successful organization, you can be totally confident that things will be done properly at the appropriate time, leaving you free to concentrate on the big picture. Never underestimate the strategic importance of good people!

This is an issue I kept returning to in the TV series. It was startlingly clear, every time, that the single major issue involved in getting the businesses back on their feet was getting the right person at the top. It goes without saying that this person then had to employ good people and motivate them. It is astonishing how often people simply fail to use this as the starting-point in any recovery. While experienced leaders will do this almost automatically, there are real, practical ways in which you can learn to build up a superb work-force. This chapter is about finding – and keeping – these special people.

Finding and building a winning work-force

I've never had a conversation with you,
so I didn't really feel that I was part of a team
FACTORY WORKER, Vernon Road

Although in my experience people are rarely as bad as they have been painted, you would be very lucky indeed to discover, when you arrive in a business, that you have the best people already there, all in the right jobs. It will take a while to establish just who is performing well, who is not, who may be undermining others, who would contribute more if he were in a different position, and so on.

Your first responsibility is to get it right with your own team – those senior staff who report directly to you. It is vital to get this level operating well, so you should spend a significant amount of time examining the way they work, the quality of their work and the way they relate to other people. You should spend as much time on a one-to-one basis with them as you can so that you really get to know them. It takes a good deal of time to get past the front that people present to you as their boss, but I assure you that it is time well spent. What you are looking for is what I call 'business-intelligent' and 'life-intelligent' people, by which I mean strong characters who in the normal run of things do not feel the need to erect protective barriers around themselves and who relate well to others. You do not necessarily need to like them (although warning bells should ring if you really dislike someone), but you absolutely must be able to feel you can trust them. Trust and faith are so fundamental to all business relationships that if you have an uneasy feeling about somebody working for you, keep probing until you are either satisfied or you have asked them to move on. To ignore those underlying feelings will, I promise you, cost you dearly in terms of the success of the business.

The same applies when conducting interviews for new staff. Never, as boss, simply rubber-stamp a new appointment – either when it is for someone who will be reporting to you or someone on the next tier down. Know what you are looking for in terms of experience, skills and personal characteristics; and spend a great deal of time – at least half a day – with the strongest candidates. Give them ample opportunity to ask questions, and allow enough time for you to tell them about the company itself (part of your task, after all, is to sell the job to them). Look very carefully at their CV and be prepared to probe thoroughly and question them deeply, then deeper still. If, for example, they say they have organized a successful launch of a product, ask them to describe exactly how they went about it, what they found, what the problems were and how they overcame them. It is a natural human desire to be associated with success, but you need to discover whether the successes they claim as their own really were their own. The fact is that if you spend several hours with a person and keep your mind open you will start to pick up all sorts of things intuitively; people cannot keep up a pretence for long, and you should have a real sense by the end of the interview whether this is a person you can trust and work with, and whether they will fit in with other members of your team.

With two notable exceptions, this approach has never failed to work for me. Interestingly, both of the exceptions were Americans. They were both superb at presenting themselves. They were incredibly convincing, wonderful performers – and turned out to be totally hopeless in practice! I believe that Americans come out of the womb with an inbuilt ability to present well. I fell for them hook, line and sinker. It is alarming, and I mean no disrespect by this, but my antenna obviously doesn't work with our friends across the pond. If you have similar blind spots be very careful, and get someone else to double-check your hunches.

There are various theories about building up teams, and balancing one person's strengths with another person's weaknesses. If you really want to, you can read up about different types of teams, different styles of behaviour and different personality types. But not in this book. Let's face it, we already know that some people are creative and free-spirited, others solid and dependable, while some like working alone, some thrive on pressure, some are conscientious, some are indecisive. All very interesting, but rather pointless. In reality, the fundamental point is that you are looking for people to 'buy into' your vision for the business and carry out their tasks in a straightforward manner. Behaviour is more important than presentation. So forget trying to manipulate people into the 'perfect' team; concentrate on finding the best possible people at this vital senior level and you will find that they will work together as a team. Decent, bright people nearly always interrelate well and – unless they are in direct competition for a role – do want each other to succeed. Furthermore, if your top level is rock solid you will almost certainly attract and keep good people all the way down through the system. Conversely, making a mistake at this level is phenomenally costly.

Encouraging teamwork, motivating your people

Make Everyone a Winner
SIGN ON THE WALL IN VERNON ROAD (DEFACED)

At the same time, I would not advise you to ignore the real ways of keeping
your team together just because you have found a great bunch of people.
One of the most important aspects of this is communication – indeed it is so
crucial that I have devoted an entire chapter – Chapter 6 – to the subject.
People need to take on board your vision for the company, and do whatever
it is you have laid out for them. You must convey what you are doing with
the business, and what they should be doing. If they have been involved in
the decision-making process that leads to a period of change, so much the
better. Another factor is consistency. I keep harking back to this key part of
leadership, and when it comes to keeping your people 'on side' it is vital.
People hate insecurity and change, and there is huge comfort to be gained
from consistency. They need to know that there is a purposeful, positive
leader in charge, that the business is on track, that the organization's rules
and regulations are fair, and that once decisions are made they are adhered
to. Aside from these two points, there are plenty of other activities and
principles that can be employed to foster team spirit and keep your work-
force with you. Remember that people desperately want to feel part of
something, and they want to feel proud of it. It is rare for anyone to seek out
isolation, and good feelings are really not that hard to engender if you are
sincere about doing things.

If he wants a good company and wants
to be successful, he's got to make sure
that he gets the work-force behind him
SEAN, Vernon Road

● Sit down together

I think that if we had regular
meetings with the various

departmental managers, possibly
things would run a little smoother.
It would make people more enthusiastic
PHIL, Arrow Ford

You should be holding monthly meetings with each individual (see page 130), but it is also important to have a monthly get-together with the whole team to encourage sharing of information and to develop a sense that you are all working together. This is a good opportunity to address head-on any friction that you are aware of: if you know that one person disagrees with a new project or a decision that another one has taken, say so in a friendly, non-confrontational manner, and actively encourage open, blame-free discussion. This is also a way of ensuring that there are no deeper, underlying problems. You are aiming for collaboration, not confrontation.

● Regular dialogue with the boss

The knowledge that you can go and talk to the boss must permeate right through the organization. A leader may (and possibly should) have an air of mystique, but one who is detached and unavailable is hard to get excited about. I have written at length about the characteristics of a leader in Chapter 1, and those that are most important for the crucial people-side of the job are to be friendly, approachable and helpful. Keep asking questions so that you get to the bottom of what a person is trying to communicate to you, and really listen to the answers. Don't be a cardboard cut-out; be human! People at every level should feel that if they have a problem or need help they are free to speak to you if necessary, or at the least to their own manager. There must be mutual respect and trust, space for disagreement and for debate, so that when a matter is resolved and a decision is made people are all prepared to pull in the same direction. Learn everyone's names, too. I am useless at this, so before every meeting I make sure that I have got them in my head.

People are starting to not even
bother with their work ... they used
to care. Trust: that's what they

*want from Richard, and that's
what they're not getting*
FACTORY WORKERS, Vernon Road

● Build project-specific teams

It can be a good idea to select three or four people from different
disciplines, who do not normally work together, to form a project team, the
purpose of which is, for example, to research a new initiative and present
their findings to the group. It should, of course, be a real project that has a
genuine chance of being taken on. In this way you achieve 'cross-fertilization'
of ideas, and can smooth over any antagonistic feelings that have arisen
purely because the people concerned have not been able to relate to each
other on a personal level. It is also a great way of making things happen.

● New initiatives

If there is something big that affects the entire business, develop a buzz about
it and get everyone pulling in the same direction. This happened at Granada
when we were researching the feasibility of taking over Trust House Forte. Lots
of people throughout the organization were involved, even in small ways, in
finding out about the business, and the real excitement this engendered led to
a great sense of togetherness. Use opportunities to help people to see how the
work they do fits in with the company's objectives.

● Stamp out negativity and don't knock others

*Morale is low, perhaps because
my morale is low and it sort of
permeates through the building*
ROBIN HARRIS, Arrow Ford

If you have any sense of rumours developing or of any unpleasantness, back-
biting or power struggles, or if you hear anyone discussing anyone else in a
negative manner, act immediately. One 'trick' I have used to good effect is to

tell one party, usually the one you suspect may be behind the problems, that the other person thinks he is fantastic. Then I stand back and watch that person go out of his way to prove that he is worthy of this accolade. Hey presto, two new friends. It helps to reduce office politics if you discourage status symbols and does so even more if you flatten hierarchies, making people feel more equal with their colleagues. The busier people are, the happier they are. If they are underemployed they all too easily fall back on their very human instincts of fear and insecurity, because they feel that their livelihoods are at stake. This is very damaging to morale. Hone your skills for picking up 'bad vibes' and deal with the problem straight away. One happy side-effect of being approachable and friendly is that through the informal chats you have with people around the office you can be in control of the rumour grapevine, rather than being scuppered by it. Never, ever knock others. Even when people leave the company, resist the temptation to blame them for mistakes that have been made.

It's a bit depressing, but that's
County Linen
WORKER, County Linen

● Career development

Gerry has prompted me to get up
and do something ... I'd like to see
people who work for us given the
chance to develop a bit more
DOROTHY, The Old Manor Hotel

After eight years of constantly
approaching him and recommending
things ... I've just gone a bit flat
Jo, Arrow Ford

Each individual needs to feel that he is either progressing within the company, or that he has the opportunity to do so and to develop as a person.

I'm talking real opportunities here, not just the odd training-day, and you have to convey this. People must know that it is possible to move up the ladder if they perform well. Status, ego and job titles are also important. These non-financial motivators are often more important to individuals than the money. I'm not talking about creating silly job titles that have no meaning; I'm urging you to pick good, exciting titles where this is possible. Plan for succession for key jobs – pinpoint possible candidates ahead of time. People will feel more fulfilled in their jobs if their work is varied, stretching and enjoyable. Remember that the more you ask of people, the more they will contribute and the better they will perform. Be demanding, and you will find they rise to the occasion. As a manager, you must nurture the raw talent around you. Use your one-to-one monthly meetings to help people feel they are on track and are making real progress.

● Delegating

People here are only as good as
you let them be, and they're not
given the opportunity. I believe that
people here want to do a good job
and they just need to be given
the tools to do it
SAM, Arrow Ford

One of the characteristics of a fine leader is the ability to apportion tasks to others, and to distinguish guiding and monitoring from interference. Think carefully about which decisions and actions need to be taken by you, and pass as many others as possible down the line. If delegating is done effectively it empowers people to make real progress in their careers. It gives them the opportunity to make a difference, to make their own decisions and to take responsibility for their actions. Even if they carry out tasks more slowly than you might have done, even if they make some mistakes, giving people real power is terrifically motivating. Encourage risk-taking in your subordinates: you will never discover a future leader unless people are given the freedom to get things wrong sometimes.

● Show appreciation

*The implication was that Vernon
Road employees had sunk Vernon Road*
FACTORY WORKER

*He's never been one for giving out
praise. We don't need it*
GEORGE, The Old Manor Hotel

Don't take credit for others' good work and throw blame around when things go wrong. People hate to work for anyone who does this. It is despicable and extremely harmful. Equally harmful is to assume that simply because a person is getting on with their job efficiently they need no recognition of the fact. Be generous with your praise, and even veer towards overdoing it. Catch people doing something well, and say so. Notice the good things, scribble a note, give them a quick call – and do it straight away. This is the plus side of being able to tell people that a particular piece of work is not good enough, as they know that when you do give them a pat on the back you really mean it. Do it publicly, too. The great thing is that if you, at the top of the organization, are doing this, the habit will filter right down through the business. It happens subtly, even subconsciously, but your behaviour – good or bad – has an enormous effect on the entire company. I saw this happen in Meridien Hotels, part of Granada at the time, when Antoine Cau was appointed to the role of its chief executive. He was superb at genuinely thanking people, and as a result staff at all levels felt terrific about working there. There is no question that people feel better about themselves when they believe that what they are doing is good and worthwhile, and when they feel they are improving their skills. Under Antoine, each tier of management became better at praising its subordinates, with motivation and performance levels increasing as a result. This, for me, was yet another example of how quickly corporate culture changes dramatically for the better, once the right boss is in charge. Remember that what you do is far more powerful than what you say, and the cost of not showing appreciation is vast.

*Do you reward someone for doing
the job they're meant to do in the
first place? No. And I don't expect
them to do it to me either*
ALISTAIR CLARK, The Old Manor Hotel

*My daughters keep telling me to
go and pat so-and-so on the back*
ROBIN, Arrow Ford

*I thank them every night before they
go home, I pat them on the back as
much as I can, then when I need to give
them a boot up the backside they know
they're having it for good reasons*
NIGEL, Arrow Ford

*I turned my back on [Robin].
He said, 'What are you doing?' I said,
'Oh, sorry, I thought you were going
to pat me on the back'*
NIGEL, Arrow Ford

● Celebrate annual results

Make a big splash when the annual results are announced. You can do this
even if your business is a small private company. You may not be able to
afford a lavish reception at a smart hotel with all the paraphernalia of
showbiz (as we were able to do at Coca-Cola and Granada), but do use what
you have creatively. Pay attention to the detail of the day. Seek to make sure
that people feel you are all doing something well, that you are all working
for an organization that is going somewhere, and send your staff home on a
huge high. Success breeds success: once the business starts to turn in good
results you will find that the excitement and commitment this generates will
produce even better ones next year.

● Team-building weekends

Whatever you do, don't dump people in a field and tell them to build a boat and go white-water rafting in it. While some love enforced team-building sessions, many people hate them, but everyone generally loves socializing and they want to have fun. So, do get people 'off site', encourage them to mix with colleagues they may not know, and to relax and socialize a little. It is such a simple thing, but breaking down the barriers between people who work in the same organization but do not know each other can have a fantastic effect – just think how we naturally mistrust people whom we do not know. Arrange to give a very short business presentation if you wish, but be honest about the purpose of the weekend and don't pretend that it is for anything other than getting to know each other. If the business has done well and people have been working particularly hard, or if you are recovering from a period of change and redundancies, take them somewhere special and invite partners too. People are always happier if their partners understand their business and appreciate what goes on at work.

● Treat people like human beings

*I don't think there's any sort of
compassion here*
Jo, Arrow Ford

*He makes people tense. It runs
better when he's not here*
MEMBER OF STAFF, The Old Manor Hotel

I am saddened that I even need to make this point, but it is certainly not the case that all organizations up and down the country are looking after their people properly. People are not pawns for you to move around on your company's chessboard without thinking about the implications. They are not there simply to perform tasks and go home at night. They have moods, ambitions, hopes, dreams, holidays, illnesses, children, parents, plans for the future, and of course, like all of us, a whole collection of everyday problems.

They have also chosen to work for you, and that may have involved sacrifices on their part – a long journey to work, complex childcare arrangements, rejection of another job or promotion elsewhere, even a cut in salary. Work is only an extension of normal relations between themselves and others; the job they do for you is only a part of their particular universe, and you cannot expect them to hang the rest of their lives up with their coats when they arrive each morning. So be aware of the real human pressures on each of the people who works for you, recognize the things that are important to them. Allow career breaks, paternity leave, sabbaticals and study leave. Don't just pretend to care; be generous and kind when people are ill or suffering family problems. Talk to them, send flowers, write personal notes, and give time off if they need it. There is nothing harder than trying to put a brave face on things and do your job normally when there are problems at home. Nit-picking and rigid adherence to rules such as statutory sickness allowance will do you no favours in the long run, and you will find that colleagues of your troubled member of staff will, more often than not, rally round and fill in. But when the person returns, expect as high a standard of work from them as you always have.

*I'm going to give [the job] my best
shot. I'm looking forward to doing
it, giving my input and not being
slammed down ... You've got to ask [him],
'Why can't we do that?'*
DOROTHY, The Old Manor Hotel

● Be fair

There is nothing worse than a 'them and us' approach to management, whereby senior players are treated in a totally different way from those lower down the organization. Make sure that things like holidays, sickness benefits, pensions, complaints procedures and so on are fair and open. Make sure too that systems and processes in place throughout the organization offer the same type of deal, whether you are the managing director or the caretaker. Of course you will have different salary scales and different perks for each position, but make sure that they are open and known to all.

● Salaries

Money can be the lousiest motivator on God's earth. Obviously people need to be remunerated according to industry standards (make sure you are fully aware of what these are), and if you are way below these you will lose people and fail to attract the best candidates. Getting the money right is important, but people often consider elements such as good working conditions, a friendly atmosphere, a sense of being appreciated and looked after – all the intangible benefits, in fact, that this chapter is about – to be far more important than an extra 10 per cent at the end of the year. Be open about what people earn at each level: you cannot hope to keep salaries secret, and it gives people something to aim for.

● Bonuses and commission

Commission arrangements work well for certain types of job, such as salespeople or factory workers, but if you have a bonus system for senior executives, scrap it. Bonuses destabilize a business: you have endless arguments about their fairness, and even if they are earned you can have a rush of resignations after bonus time as people cash in and move on. Senior figures will always try to reduce their financial targets in order to ensure they receive a bonus for meeting them, thus reducing the ambition of the organization. Bonuses can be unfair on some sections in the business who may have been affected by outside factors; and if a bonus is less one year than the next, unhelpful comparisons and grumblings are bound to arise. Scrap bonuses and save a huge amount of angst and time. Instead, be prepared to increase pay dramatically for first-class people you really want to keep.

Each department has its own cost centre,
and everyone is trying to ... get a bonus
for their department. There seems to be
some animosity between Rapid Fit and
Service as we are fighting for the same work
Jo, Arrow Ford

● Performance problems

*They come to work when they've
got nothing else to do*
TIM MOORE, County Linen

Part of building effective teams, and the plus side of being able to show appreciation for good work, is addressing performance problems. Don't wait until the annual appraisal (better still, don't have an annual appraisal). Deal with any difficult issues immediately. The moment you notice something serious – shoddy work, a sustained drop in the figures, an unhappy customer – take it up with the person concerned and ask them exactly what happened. There may be a perfectly innocent explanation, in which case accept it and move on. If the problem has been caused by a simple lack of skills, then address this with training. If the excuses do not stack up, set a time frame for improvement and specify exactly what that improvement should be. Be prepared to be pleasantly surprised: a little honest concern expressed in time can produce massively improved results. On the other hand, it is lethal to shy away from problems about performance. Firstly other colleagues may wonder why you are failing to address an issue; secondly, your awareness of substandard work will affect your ability to deal with the individual. Resentment will build up, and at some point you will blow. The saddest side of dealing with poor performance, and the hardest to deal with, is when someone is giving their utmost to the job yet is simply not up to it. You must grasp the nettle, remove them from the role in which they are failing and genuinely try to find another position for them.

*I don't like people not liking me, and
sometimes you have got to be cruel in
business. It is much easier to hire
somebody than fire somebody.
It is very difficult to do the bad
things in a company which you need
to do in order to keep it going*
ROBIN, Arrow Ford

● Forgiving genuine mistakes

People must also be allowed to make mistakes and be forgiven – rather like the truth and reconciliation process in post-apartheid South Africa, which I admired tremendously. It may seem a strange comparison to make, but there is a true virtue in business in asking for a full confession, being merciful, and drawing a line. It assists in building a culture of openness and honesty, stops resentment and bitterness building up, and enables people to learn from their mistakes and move forward positively.

● Reverse headhunting

Keep in touch with good people who leave your organization – you may need to re-employ them at some point. It is healthy for them to leave, learn new skills with a competitor, and return to the fold. It is also reassuring for other staff to see that yours is a company that people wish to come back to.

Making *I'll Show Them Who's Boss* was a fascinating process, not least for the insight it gave me into how the people side of a business is managed (or not) in small to medium-sized firms. Naturally there were complex family relationships which had a huge impact on the interactions between people, and I will look at these in chapter 7. Here I will concentrate on those companies that had a sizeable work-force and staff with whom I was able to talk. On the occasions we managed to identify a clear leader, invariably that individual had people skills as well as an innate business sense.

* * *

Simon at **George Brown & Sons** was brilliant on the people side, and that was partly why he was the obvious choice for managing director. He was very clear about the relative strengths and weaknesses of the other people in the company, and had the ability to act on this knowledge. He could see which people were in the wrong jobs (and there were several) but could make a greater contribution in other positions, he identified who was ripe for promotion, and he undertook his reshuffle quickly and sensibly. This cannot have been easy, particularly as he was dealing with older family members, but he handled it very well. Simon's friendly but firm style and his passion for improving the business have filtered through the company. Now the atmosphere has changed markedly, people have much more of a spring in their step, there is a great buzz about the future, and much more of a sense that these people are all enthusiastic about working together. In 2004 the company started to work towards the 'Investors in People' award.

* * *

At the opposite extreme was Richard Chaplin of **Vernon Road**, who had some difficulties when it came to dealing with people. As a manager he often lacked consistency and clarity, and a culture of blame had grown up. As a result there was little team spirit, a definite 'them and us' feeling, a lack of trust, certainly no praise – and hence scant motivation to produce good-quality merchandise. To whip up improved performance, Richard's approach was to dragoon the workers. Belatedly, he did realize that he needed to have the staff with him, and he was able to give rousing speeches. Sadly, reality did not reflect what he claimed, and with his continual changes of mind he forfeited the workers' trust. 'It's the uncertainty, isn't it? The fact that you never know what's coming next,' said one of them ruefully. Ironically, when pushed, Richard did have an ability to humble himself and appeal to the staff on a human level – but his antagonistic persona kept setting him back. The business was doomed, and you can find out what happened in chapters 4 and 6.

* * *

Alistair Clark, the hard, driven boss at the **The Old Manor Hotel,** Fife, was a very strong leader with an excellent business nose. His downfall was on the people side: the staff were afraid of him on account of his domineering manner, his tendency to bark instructions, his intolerance of mistakes, his unwillingness to show appreciation, and his fiercely high standards. Surprisingly, the business was successful despite all this, but his sons had not dared tackle him on the tricky issue of his retirement. Anyone with good people skills, such as Alistair's wife Dorothy, found them used to douse flames rather than resolve genuine issues. One son admitted that the antagonism between father and sons did actually spark a huge release of energy, a reaction which can sometimes be therapeutic, but in this case I felt it did more harm than good. Alistair was such a perfectionist, too, and knew he had such good business judgement, that he found it almost impossible to delegate – another reason why his sons had had no space to develop their own skills and careers. I felt he had very little awareness of people's needs, and when I talked to him about his lack of ability to show appreciation he was amazed that it was such a major issue for people, but nevertheless decided to adopt 'pat on the back' as a new strategy. I think that by the time we left he was making real progress towards taking a kinder, gentler approach to the people in his business. Eventually – with the two sons in charge, and with Dorothy running the human resources side – I believed the company would be in good shape to face the future in a more balanced and rounded way, with happier, more relaxed staff.

* * *

At the Welsh car dealership, **Arrow Ford**, communication was disastrous. Robin Harris was a poor manager of people: he was distant, unavailable and depressed. So bad were his communication skills that he sometimes went off on holiday without informing people he was going, leaving no one in charge! He rarely praised anyone, or noticed if they were working well. There were few meetings, little follow-up on initiatives, no sharing of news, minimal dissemination of financial information – yet he was asking people to 'do their best'. How could they? It was extremely unfair to ask this of them without defining what he was looking for. None of the five departments had a clear idea of the pressures on each other, nor of the opportunities for co-operation. There was a good deal of internal strife. There was little sense of teamwork, although certain individuals did enjoy their jobs. There were no clear career paths, no proper systems and procedures, and his daughters were being held back from progressing in their careers. I was surprised that the business had managed to stay afloat for so long, although I suspected it was due in large part to the buoyant car market in the 1990s. When we arrived to try to help, it was clear that in an increasingly tough market the lack of management and consequent low morale were having a disastrous effect on the profits. Part of the business, however, was rather more successful. It was run by a different boss, Nigel Bond, who had a completely different attitude towards his staff. He made a point of always being available for them, he used financial incentives and doled out praise liberally; and he expected – and achieved – high standards. That is why I knew he would make such a terrific new leader.

* * *

One of the things that worried me about Henry at **Norwood Park** was a kind of swagger and youthful arrogance that his father did not have. There were comments from some staff I spoke to that led me to believe that Henry was generally liked but not respected, and that he had had some problems with the staff and had upset some members of the golf club. I suspect that Sir John misguidedly felt that Henry would continue his own gentle, hands-off management style as opposed to a more ruthless, professional approach that someone like Suzannah might introduce. Henry knew he did not have the mandate of all his siblings to run the business, and as a result he felt observed and hemmed in. Again – not a good start for rallying the troops. One can only hope that as he matures Henry will develop and hone his people skills.

* * *

It was clear from the anger that greeted Anthony and Tim of **County Linen** on their walkabout tours of the two factories that neither brother had mastered the crucial art of dealing with people. They were not regarded with much respect by their staff, who felt free to express their frustration with the way they were being managed. Morale was dangerously low, no one seemed to take any pride in their work, and relations between the two plants were so strained that on at least one occasion the police had to be called to break up a fight at the Christmas party. Anthony admitted he had not held any shift meetings with his managers for two years, and Tim was told he never listened. They were accused of being inconsistent and partisan: it was clear that there was a huge gulf between the management and workers. Yet neither brother apologised nor admitted any fault – like Richard Chaplin of Vernon Road their first response was to blame the workers. It is my belief that failure is always the fault of the management. The workers, as a result, were so suspicious of management that even when Anthony presented his 'gift' of the new bonus scheme to the staff there was a good deal of cynicism on the shop floor. Instead of saying, 'We're in this together and it hasn't been working, for which I take full responsibility. I apologise for what you have been going through, but from here on in we are really going to do something great with this company,' what it sounded like was this: 'You haven't done very well, but I'm giving you another chance if you work harder.' That was not calculated to reduce the fear of job losses that permeated the company, and fear is more harmful to a business than paying out any extra bonuses. Standing up in front of the entire staff has a phenomenal impact and should only be done when a leader is totally prepared. If only Anthony had waited until he had thought through changes in management and procedures, and presented these as a one-off road to recovery, he would have had a much better chance of inspiring staff and starting afresh. In fact, when – two months after making the announcement – no bonus payments had been made, it was clear that the situation was even worse than before. As one of the shop-floor managers commented: 'It's going to be, I think, now impossible to get people back to believing what we're doing. It's made my job harder.'

Such was the state of morale in the company that I suggested it would be best for someone to come in from outside to take the business forward. It seemed almost too good to be true when Gordon Dick – associated in the minds of many of the staff with the former period of prosperity – came forward as a possible contender for the position of chairman. He was the key figure I had been looking for: someone of substance, good at follow-through, and someone who knew how to approach people.

CHAPTER FOUR

Doing the dirt

Do it once – and do it well

Over the course of my business career, I have been fortunate enough to have had the opportunity to be in a position to turn many companies and organizations around. In fact I believe that there is nothing more exciting for a business leader than to have the chance to take something which is in a mess, shake it up, sort it out and make it better. In Chapter 2 I outlined part of this process: the steps involved in working out a strategy for your business that will ensure greater efficiency and profitability, and the action plans that inevitably follow. While you will have explored various ways in which you might sell more of what you produce (broadly speaking), a key part of the process you will have gone through is looking in great detail at the financial side of your operation, so you should have a picture of what, if any, cost savings need to be made. And cost savings often mean redundancies.

Very often businesses become flabby and unfit over a period of time. We may not always recognize it, but working in a business like this is rarely a satisfying experience. Any enforced reduction of staffing levels is painful, and it is inevitable that when this is done a business goes through an unpleasant and difficult time. I know I have gained a reputation as a ruthless hirer and firer, but I believe that it is far better to work for a successful, happy operation that is making money, than for an overstaffed, depressing business that is going down the pan.

You will know from the previous chapter how firmly I believe in treating your people well. Sadly, there is nothing that will make the reality of redundancy sweet for those at the receiving end of it, but there are ways of helping them through the process humanely. This chapter will lay out in detail how best to do this, and will warn you what not to do.

Staff cuts are a reality of modern business life, and if there are times when they simply have to be made, the kindest and best thing for all concerned is to do it once, do it quickly, do it well, and look after the remaining staff by going on to make the company successful. For only successful companies represent a stable base for future employment.

Knowing when to do it

It seems to me that the number of people tends to increase within an organization more quickly than there are jobs. Left to their own devices, departments never voluntarily cut themselves back; rather, they grow larger and busier, and in their busy-ness little thought is given to how much they usefully contribute. In the belief that their power and pay are related to the number of people that report to them, managers increase staffing levels and build mini empires. When people leave they are replaced, so it is the natural process for an organization to become a huge, sprawling monster full of busy people working hard but contributing less and less to the success of the business. However, when a company is doing really well, it is better not to rock the boat by making people redundant just to save a few bob here and there. Obviously, you need to keep an eye on certain housekeeping matters (which might mean not replacing someone who leaves, and removing or moving those who are genuinely in the wrong jobs), but there will always be a certain amount of fat around. The real challenges come when the business is in trouble.

It is really not that hard to spot the early signs of serious trouble if you bother to look objectively. If turnover is down, profits are down, orders are down, new customers are few, and your direct competitors are doing better than you are – then, for heaven's sake, don't ignore this. Don't blame it on the market or someone else; acknowledge that you have a problem. There may, of course, be genuine industry-specific or wider economic factors affecting you and, in truth, there is not much you can do to alter these. As part of your strategy review exercise, look hard at the figures and extrapolate from them to see where you will be if you do nothing. It is up to you to refuse to accept a clear downward trend, and to seek help. Never accept that there is nothing you can do to save the company, unless it has already collapsed. If there is life still there, you should be able to find financial backing to get things up and running again, because it is in the shareholders' and bank's best interests to support your company to enable it to continue trading, but you must act quickly. That means having, among other things, a cost-cutting plan in hand.

Dos and don'ts

Once you have decided to reduce staffing levels I'm afraid you will find, as leader, that you are on your own here. No one wants to face this, to have blood on their hands. It is possible – and indeed important – to separate the issue of having to make redundancies from how you do it and what you do for the people who are going. To help everyone get through this horrible time as cleanly as possible, and to enable the business to get back on its feet as soon as possible, make sure you do it well.

● Be as quick as you can

Morale is the life-blood of a company, and the longer you drag out a period of uncertainty and change, the worse people will feel. It is completely natural for people to worry about their futures, their families and their self-esteem, but while they have this threat to their livelihoods hanging over them they will be underperforming and the business will suffer greatly. If they are to leave, they need to know as soon as possible so that they can move on. If you delay too long people may think that the threat has disappeared, which makes it all the worse when you do drop the bomb. The entire process from initial announcement to leaving dates should be no more than eight weeks.

● Do not offer voluntary redundancies

In my view voluntary redundancy is a cowardly route. It wastes resources, and drags out the period of change, because inevitably you will need a second stage to the redundancy process. Voluntary redundancy means that those who have most to gain financially will be the ones to come forward, and as they are the people who have been there the longest, not only will you lose their valuable experience but you will be paying over the odds for them to go. This could mean the difference between survival and failure. You will also lose the best people – those who are confident of finding new employment, probably with a competitor – the very ones you need in order to survive. This is the equivalent of letting those on board a threatened ship who can do the most to rescue the others swan off on the first lifeboat. As a manager you need to have the courage to decide whom you would like to keep, and to try as far as possible to make that happen. Voluntary redundancies mean you are not in control, so don't offer them. If the rules say you must, then see if you can change them.

● Do not consult lawyers

It is too costly in terms of time, not to mention money. Lawyers will always give you safe advice, lots of 'on the one hand' stuff. In a dire situation I would rather risk making the odd mistake than spend months in legalese. In a large organization you are almost bound to get some things wrong, although in fact I have never had anything of significance rebound back on me. Utilize your own human resources department – its staff should know all the basics, and be aware of any union requirements and last in, first out issues. In fact, if they don't, they have failed and should perhaps feature on the redundancy list.

● Overdo it

Even if you think you are overdoing it, you are probably not. Even I, reputedly the most Draconian head-count reducer of recent history, have never gone far enough. There is always such strong resistance – people will fight for themselves, and for their staff. This is only natural, as is your own wish to minimize job losses and the resultant human misery. In any case it is a one-way bet, because if, as a result of slightly overdoing it, you later need to build up staff levels, that will be seen as a positive step in the recovery process.

When is he going to get it right?
When we've all been made redundant?
They keep telling me to be positive,
but how can I be positive when I
don't know what they're doing at the top?
FACTORY WORKER, Vernon Road

● Do it once

I cannot overemphasize the importance of this – it is crucial to get all this nasty business over with cleanly, and move on. If you have to come back and do it again you will do a great deal of harm. I have seen companies fail because they have had several waves of redundancies, each of which loses more and more trust, causing morale to fall to such a level that recovery is nearly impossible.

There's a lot of bad feeling at the
minute. A lot of bad feeling
FACTORY WORKER, Vernon Road

● Be generous

Within the bounds of commercial viability, and remembering that your purpose is to save costs, you should be generous – in terms of both financial remuneration and useful advice to those who have lost their jobs.

Everybody whose name is on the
list stay behind, and if your name
is not on the list ... you're finished
at Vernon Road
FACTORY WORKER, Vernon Road

● Don't be paranoid

There is nothing crueller and more damaging to ongoing morale than giving out bin liners and making people clear their desks on the day they receive the news. Give them a bit of time, and don't panic that they might filch office supplies, client details or a list of hot prospects. If they were going to do this, I can almost guarantee that they will already have done it.

He's been in the company less than
twelve months and he's ... just made
people redundant as if they didn't matter
FACTORY WORKER, Vernon Road

I just hope he don't f*** up any
more lives because he's f***ed
enough up as it is
FACTORY WORKER, Vernon Road

Moving on, moving up

There are, to my mind, five clear steps to take in order to ensure that a redundancy programme is implemented cleanly, kindly and efficiently:

1 Making the Announcement
As soon as possible after you have drawn up your outline plan and have decided on the best courses of action in each area, announce to the staff that there will be a period of change that will involve making some people redundant. Give them a date by which the decisions will be made, which should never be more than a fortnight after the initial announcement. A week is better.

2 Drawing Up the List
Ask each line manager to make specific cost savings by producing a list of people from his team to be made redundant (along with other cost-saving measures). Specify the percentage amount you need to cut from the salary bill. You cannot do it for him, as he will be the only person who knows enough about each individual concerned. He will know who is busy but not contributing, who is pleasant but underperforming, and who is good,

motivated and valuable. This will be extremely hard for people – no manager will feel happy doing this, even if he can see the sense in it. You should help them by taking the responsibility on your own shoulders, and – in a way – giving them no choice but to do it. In carrying out this exercise you should try as far as possible to work with those who are staying with the company. If, however, you already know that a line manager will be going, tell them up front and let them know when and on what terms, before they put their own list together. Give a deadline for completion of this list of no more than a week.

3 Working Out the Deal
Make sure that your human resources staff work out exactly what the deal for each person will be, right down to the most minute detail such as compensation for holidays not taken. You need to have everything covered, so that you can give full and accurate information to people on the day they are spoken to.

4 Doing the Deed
Inform all the people who are being made redundant on the same day, preferably early in the week. If this is not possible, make sure that it does not take more than two days. Speak to all the senior executives yourself, and have the line managers deal with their own staff. It is very important for people to be informed by their direct boss, and the interview should be conducted as firmly and as kindly as possible. I have seen it done very badly – people being informed by text message, workers told to check a list to see if they are in or out, people hearing from others that they have lost their job.

There are certain issues you absolutely must cover in your meetings with the people concerned. First of all, apologise. Then be honest and clear in explaining the following:

- Be honest about the financial constraints on the company and the need to make cost savings.
- Explain the fact that the individual has been selected for redundancy and this decision is non-negotiable.

- Don't be afraid of allowing someone to express their anger or sorrow, but stay calm and firm yourself. You may find many people are strangely relieved, now that you are giving them a firm decision.
- Tell them which day they will be leaving, how much they will be paid, what happens to their holiday entitlements, expense claims, pension, car and other perks – absolutely every detail should be covered.
- If there are positions available within the company it is far better to offer them to specific individuals on the day you can. If that is impossible, but there are jobs that the person might apply for, let them know what the jobs are, when the interviews are, and how exactly to go about applying for them.
- Let them know if you are offering career or emotional counselling and, if so, how this will work for them, who will contact them and when. Make absolutely sure the counselling happens.

People will be in shock, and will not be able to remember much of what you have said. However, they will need to go home to their partners and explain what has happened, and they need to start planning for their futures. It is vital, therefore, at the end of each interview, to hand the individual a letter that covers all these points. If you are going to offer a reference, tell them, so that they can use it accordingly.

5 Boosting Morale

To go back to my earlier point about morale, the final step in the process is to reassure the remaining staff. It is vital, on the same day that you announce the redundancies, to pay attention to those who are staying. They need to believe that this was a one-off exercise, and that the business is now in a position to get back into good financial shape. Send a letter out to all staff, explaining what has happened, and drawing a line to mark the end of uncertainty and the beginning of a new era. Be as positive and upbeat as you can, bearing in mind that people will still be feeling upset and shaken. Above all, the letter should be honest, and feel honest. It could be along these lines:

Dear ....

Today we have announced x redundancies within the company. Those directly involved have been informed this morning and it has been agreed that they will leave this Friday.

I am sorry that this has proved necessary, but it is clear to me that we could not continue to sustain losses at the current level and survive.

However, now that we have taken this difficult step, it is clear that we have a much stronger base from which to move forward. We will now set out to bring the company back to full strength and I very much look forward to working with you to that end.

Yours, etc

As soon as the dust has settled, it is a good idea to hold a 'rally the troops' meeting at which you address all staff and present your plans for moving the business forward. This is your chance to be really positive and inspiring, and get 'hearts and minds' backing for turning the business around.

This is what happened at Granada. As a direct result of my review (see pages 63–71) I forced the entire organization to look at where cut-backs could be made, and sadly within two months we had made over one thousand people redundant. Although this was deeply unpleasant for all concerned, everyone was given the news in a straightforward, honest way by their direct manager, and everyone was given a letter laying out how it affected them. Until the redundancies were made, morale was very low and it was undeniably a difficult period. I came in for a huge amount of flak over some of the television redundancies, but I stuck to my guns and tried to put my side of the story across in as honest and human a way as possible. Although I knew that, fundamentally, people did want to get the nasty business over with, and get on with things, I was amazed to see quite how quickly the mood lifted when the redundancies were over. In the first year we were able to declare results that were 10 per cent up on what the market expected. This gave a huge boost to staff (but you can only do this once!). They knew that there would be no more redundancies and that they were part of a team that was going to make a success out of the business. Almost overnight Granada stopped being a hopeless case and started becoming a success story. This was because we got the numbers broadly right, the timing right, and the big thrust afterwards right.

Earlier in my career I had used the same approach to produce similar turnarounds at Grand Met Contract Services and at their Coca-Cola franchise. At Grand Met Contract Services I spent two months travelling around the various parts of the business, many of which were in the Middle East, making judgements about what was working and what wasn't, and what might be made to work if it were done differently. Yes, it took some harsh decisions but, by paying attention to those areas where there was real potential, we were able to grow the business anew. Over just two years the business, which had been losing £7 million, produced a profit of £17 million. At Coca-Cola Southern Bottlers there was a hugely overstaffed finance department which needed to be reduced, and a thin sales and marketing department which needed to be beefed up. I always believe it is important to have as many people as possible in positions that have a direct effect on the business – pulling in customers, making sales; and as few people in the administration areas as are necessary to do the job. Coca-Cola had not made a profit in four years, and in my first year as managing director it made a profit of £3.2 million.

It was a rather different story when I became chairman of the Arts Council. This was an unwieldy, amorphous, inefficient organization. When I arrived to sort it out I felt like an alien being from another world. The redundancies happened at two levels. Firstly, there was the council itself, made up of twenty volunteers who all agreed that change was needed and all resigned at my request after our first meeting. They were not quite so compliant when I failed to reappoint most of them, but that was a storm I knew I had to ride out. Secondly, there was the organization itself, and this is where I made my big mistake. There was a voluntary redundancy policy in place, which I went along with. As a result, it took six or seven months before we knew who was going and who was staying. First we had a delay while people decided whether to take voluntary redundancy, then each available position had to be advertised internally. Further interviews then had to be conducted. Needless to say, morale was low. While this uncertainty hung over people, it was nearly impossible to get on and achieve things for the arts in England, and much needed to be done. It was a messy, time-consuming and costly process and, with my background, I couldn't believe that I had allowed myself to become involved in it. I have no doubt that it would have been much kinder and more decent to draw up a list, give people the bad news, and have them out a few days later – people are always much better off if they know where they stand. I regret to this day not having insisted on taking the corporate route and simply getting on with it.

My whole aim was to make the Arts Council more effective, and I believe it now works very well. In the past, people applying for funding would have had to wait months for a decision; now they receive a quick and clear one. There are only four funding schemes, rather than some two hundred. There is only one body involved, rather than eleven separate organizations, and the system is the same everywhere throughout England. As a direct result of these initiatives we received a huge increase in funding for the arts – something which I believe was long overdue.

When I started to tackle the problems faced by the businesses in *I'll Show Them Who's Boss*, I usually found that the solution lay with the boss himself. Making staff cut-backs was not an issue for most of these businesses, mainly because the leaders had not got to first base in planning for long-term profitability. There was one business, however, where redundancies were very much the order of the day, and I don't think I have ever seen them handled in a worse way.

Richard and Henry Chaplin went from a business that itself had problems, and bought a bigger, albeit bankrupt one. In acquiring **Vernon Road** Richard acquired the work-force along with it. When I arrived on the scene, the workers were unmotivated, and Richard was furious. I tried very hard to get a true picture of the company's financial situation and was convinced by the owners that they had 'orders coming out of their ears', and that the only problem was the volume of 'returns', due to poor-quality work by the work-force. When Richard tried to induce staff to turn out textiles without marks, cuts, holes and snags, his approach was to instruct them to work harder. He told them in no uncertain terms what to do and how to do it – yet it simply didn't get done. He once asked me, 'What do you do with people who are either not listening to you or believe that what you're telling them is wrong? Do you give them written warnings? Do you sack them?' The answer, really, was that he was starting from the wrong place. The workers did not trust him, because they felt he had misled them so often, and therefore were not prepared to work hard for him. A pep talk helped make people feel more positive, but business didn't improve. Richard sold off some machinery and his own car in order to raise extra cash, but eventually decided to make twelve people redundant – some of whom had only recently been employed. I tried to get him to make sure that he did it right, including doing more than he thought he needed to do. In a move that was disastrous for morale, he sent Jeff Mason to give the news to some of the remaining workers (see page 141). Jeff, totally out of touch with feelings on the shop floor, reported that the news was well received. After this, I persuaded Richard that it was time to let Jeff go.

I helped Richard to see that this was a golden opportunity to get the remaining workers behind him, persuade them their jobs were safe and get them to work even harder. The speech he made to them was an amazing performance.

> It is a year today that we actually took over and started running Vernon Road, but we've achieved an awful lot. Do you all understand, you know, what we have actually done? We've got this business back to where it should be, and I thank you for that, and each one of you should feel proud that you've actually achieved that, but I know that it's been with a lot of hardships. And I do truly appreciate what you have been going through because it must be hell to not know whether you've got a job from one day to the next, and I know staff morale has been low. I know it's been very low. I've taken steps to try and sort that out.
>
> Now, we've made the hardest decision of our business career today, and I think it's already probably gone round the work-force that we've actually let Mr Mason go; he's no longer here. This guy has worked with me and my father for the best part of twenty-five, thirty years so it's almost like letting a brother or a son go. It's a huge step but I've listened to what you've said, I've listened to what other people have said and taken the action that I deemed was needed at this moment in time.
>
> There are going to be no more redundancies from the shop floor, the workers,

because I know people have been coming to me and saying: 'Are we going to be made redundant?' We have to make it work with what we've got here now, this is the team, you are the people, we've got to make it work with who's here now. You guys, I'm asking you to work with me to make this work. I want to stand here today and say to you this is the best work-force I've had the pleasure of working with. What I'm saying to you is now we've got the work, you've seen it, you know it's there, if we do that properly to the best of our ability customers will carry on sending that work in, because we're good. Not only are we good, we can be the best, the very best. Thank you very much.

He showed that he had listened to the work-force and taken a tough decision, and his passion for the business certainly shone through. I could see the workers being won over. I had firmly believed that the way to solve the financial problems was to have the people who were doing the job motivated to do it properly, and at this point they were finally feeling pleased and positive. I had the feeling that this could represent a real turning-point for the business. It was not to be. A week later, unbelievably, Jeff was back. I simply could not see how Richard could do something so misguided – it gave all the wrong signals to the work-force.

It was all downhill from there. A month later he decided to bring in a second wave of redundancies, and handed out a hit list of forty-four names. Some other workers also left in disgust. It was chaotic, and there was little trust left between the management and the work-force.

CHAPTER FIVE

Don't sweat the small stuff

While you're watching the pennies, someone will run off with the pounds

When you have built your business up from scratch, it is hard to know when it is time to step back from the detail and start to focus on the bigger picture. Indeed, sometimes it is hard to know what is detail and what is bigger picture. I have chosen to devote a whole chapter to this topic because when I have been picking up the pieces of businesses in trouble it has invariably been my experience that no one was looking at the big issues. They were all out scrubbing the decks while the ship was heading for the rocks. This also struck me again and again when I talked to the leaders of the businesses for the *I'll Show Them Who's Boss* series. Many of them were bogged down in ridiculous detail that was simply not worth their precious time, while the really important issues were being ignored. As a result the businesses lacked focus, direction and leadership. It was my job to help them (or their successor) to separate the big from the small and take their companies forward. The title of this chapter is borrowed from a best-selling book of that name by Richard Carlson, which I have not read as I understand that the author is very much of my own mind. In other words, that it is important to focus on the ten big things that matter, rather than diffuse your energy on two hundred little ones that – in the long run – don't. By this I don't mean that the detail of running a business is unimportant. It isn't – it's vital. But you can easily make sure that it is attended to. It is much more difficult to keep your mind on the big picture.

Our comfort zones

It is a very common and understandable human characteristic to be much more comfortable dealing with the familiar than the unknown. In a business context it means that we are happier dealing with small stuff, as we can get our minds around it – it is more concrete, and more real, and we feel we can have a direct influence and get results without having to rely on others. At every level of a business you can find people doing the easy tasks first, faffing around with unimportant but time-consuming details, worrying about tiny problems, getting involved in other people's areas. We are all drawn towards doing what we feel we are good at, and we often even try to do the jobs we used to do before we were promoted. Thus you may see sales directors still calling on customers, marketing directors writing press releases, financial directors counting the petty cash, production directors repairing a breakdown on the production line ... While they are doing these things it is impossible to think, plan and make the larger, more important decisions. This tendency to dabble in detail is sometimes called micromanaging, and I believe it is very damaging to the long-term prospects for a business. There are exceptions to this rule: some successful leaders have used an obsession for detail to good effect, while others are so involved in high-level deal-making that they are cut off from the realities of their business. The real problems come when managing directors worry about such things as the colour of the coffee cups, as happened in one of our programmes. This is horribly dangerous. If this is something you recognize in yourself it is time to stop behaving like a busy fool, stand back, and learn to see the whole wood not just the trees.

In this chapter I will set out ways of recognizing whether you are sweating your own small stuff, how to stop, and which are the few big issues you ought to be concentrating on.

The small stuff

It is partly our attitudes and working practices that we have developed over years that affect whether we are naturally able to focus on the all-important big picture. Imagine that each of the following six statements has a red light attached to it. If you can answer 'yes' to any of them, illuminate the red light in your mind. The more red lights you switch on, the more your small stuff is taking over your life, and the greater danger you are in.

1 I wish I had more people I could delegate to
2 I find it hard saying no
3 I never have enough time to do everything
4 I am afraid of making mistakes
5 Finance is not my strong point
6 I am conscientious and careful in my work
7 I don't have a strategic plan

Even if just a few of these apply to you, I'd be prepared to bet that your desk is piled high with unread documents, faxes, reports, brochures, memos and sets of figures. You work all the hours God sends, because it is the only way you can make any inroads into the huge pile of work. You wish you could pass it on to others, but you do not trust anyone else to do it as well as you can. Because you are afraid of getting something wrong, you would prefer not to do it at all, and where figures are concerned your mind goes a bit blank. The last thing you have got time to concentrate on is the future direction of your business or department, so you seek refuge in detail.

I am exaggerating, of course, but the fact is that any of these points can result in your giving too much attention to the kind of detail that should be passed down the line to someone else. As a senior manager your role is a thinking role, and you have to discipline yourself into this mindset. If you are surrounded by too many bits of paper, you're done for.

The good news, though, is that you really can force yourself into 'big picture' thinking. It is a matter of brushing up on a few key skills, being ruthless about sticking to your new rules, knowing what the few important issues are for your business and concentrating solely on them – and at the same time, of course, positively resisting the small stuff.

There's too much sugar in the flapjack
ALASTAIR, AMT Espresso

Big picture skills

● Delegation

This is the ultimate key to efficiency and the answer to small-stuff snowstorms. If you have too much on your desk, in your e-mail inbox or in your mind you must clear it out, and the best way of doing this is to entrust each routine, detailed or non-crucial task to a specific member of staff. You retain overall responsibility, and must know what you have asked of whom, and you should follow up regularly (see page 22). Brief the person fully, be specific about what you are expecting from them, and resist the urge to tell them exactly how to do it. If you can, delegate objectives, not specific activities. The person will respond to the trust you are putting in them, and even if the way they carry a task out is different to what you might have done, be sure to praise and encourage them on what they have done well, and give them constructive feedback if there is room for improvement. An inability to delegate is one of the biggest causes of paper logjams in an office, and also one of the biggest causes of disaffection among staff. They want more responsibility! They want to progress. They want to be challenged. They want to learn. Do not stand in their way. Given some responsibilities and allowed just to get on with it, they will feel better and have the sense that they are growing in their jobs.

● Saying no

As a manager you have a lot of calls on your time and attention, and each one is a potential minefield of detail and delay. If it is something you can say no to, just say it. Think of the time you will save! If you ask for more information, if you ask for someone else's opinion, if you ask for the material to be presented in a different way, or if you give any number of excuses for not coming to a decision, ask yourself why you are doing this. Are you trying to let someone down gently? Do you genuinely need more information? Decisions are often delayed and deferred as a way of not doing something you know will never happen, but the upshot is huge angst and massive waste of time and money. Be realistic, be brave, and be honest. Let it go.

● Time management

Good management of time goes hand in hand with freeing yourself up to concentrate on the big picture. If you are a poor time-manager you will get bogged down in detail. If you are bogged down in detail you will not have any time to look at the key issues. If you cannot concentrate on the key issues you are lost. In many ways time management is the underlying sub-text of this book. I want you to redefine what you spend your days doing; surround yourself with excellent subordinates; delegate effectively; speak to people directly rather than writing long memos or e-mails; have open, direct relationships with your staff; and develop a helicopter vision. Prioritize sensibly: do the most important thing first and complete it before going on to the next item. Attend essential meetings only, and be ruthless with what comes across your desk, and either bin it, pass it on or act on it (in that order).

● An organized organization

I hate military terminology, but for once it is useful here. It's a jungle out there and your business must be ready for battle. You need the best weapons, the best lieutenants, and everything must work like a well-oiled machine. It is your job to ensure that you have good processes and good systems so that the company makes its own decisions and can be in charge of the market-place rather than being at the receiving end of other people's bayonets! An organization that works well, and feels good about itself, is one that controls costs, prices cleverly and sells well. You must be in control of your destiny, on a personal and corporate level.

● Simplify your life

Don't be frightened by the idea of looking at the big picture. It is amazingly simple. Let others worry about the myriad fiddly things that make up the hugely complex machine that is your organization, close your eyes, and imagine. Your desk is clear apart from a phone, a computer and one in-tray containing the morning's post. You have one filing cabinet, and in it are no more than thirty files. One to seven contain action plans and updates for the managers who report to you. The others are about current events and should be changed as the need arises. Throw old stuff away. You prioritize your tasks for the day, you have very few meetings, if any. You spend a good deal of time talking to people and enthusing them. You take regular time off to think, to play golf, to ride horses or spend time with your family.

● Resist small stuff

And, just in case you need reminding – DON'T do the routine jobs, which I classify as:

Housekeeping: picking up the rubbish, tidying the office
Hospitality: making the coffee, getting the lunch in
Secretarial: reading e-mails, sending faxes, organizing meetings, filing
Administrative: choosing the type of fleet cars, deciding on the colour of envelopes, ordering office supplies, worrying about the type of carpet for your office or the location of pot plants
End product: getting too involved in the packaging, presentation, pricing or promotion

If you were surprised to see e-mails on this list, think again. The point about e-maisl is that most people are monitors of their own in-boxes, and e-mails come directly to their workstation. I am not disputing the fact that it can be incredibly useful to receive information this quickly and this directly. However, if you are not careful it will set the agenda for your working day. A message pops up on your screen in the same, insistent way as the phone rings. You won't know if it is small stuff or big stuff until you open it and read it. The answer is to treat an e-mail as you would any other piece of correspondence. Get someone else to screen it first.

And, above all, DON'T do other people's jobs for them – they will do them a great deal better than you, and will feel lost if you do their work for them. If you need help in lightening your own load, re-examine whether you really need to do everything that is in your in-tray and, if so, find out if anyone has any spare capacity or consider bringing in more staff.

Before you read on, make a list of the small stuff you are positively not going to do any more:

....

....

....

....

....

....

....

• Have a break

If you can, get away from the office. A holiday or even a weekend can provide a much-needed space in which to think. Even with a clear desk, a superbly efficient office, and subordinates who have swept up those tasks you no longer need to worry about doing yourself, it can be hard to achieve the distance from the day-to-day concerns that you will need in order to allow your mind to focus on big picture thinking.

Big picture thinking

There are not very many surprises in business, yet people often ask themselves how such-and-such a company did not see something coming. Thinking ahead is the prime role of the strategist/leader, and I went into this in more detail in Chapter 2. You need to develop a sixth sense about what is going on on a larger scale, and if you allow yourself to get caught up in the minutiae of running a business it will be heading for trouble. These larger-scale issues are (a) an awareness of the industry in general, and (b) the vulnerabilities of your business in particular, where you are most at risk and what the warning signs of a downturn might be.

• Trends in your industry sector

There are factors affecting your business that go far wider than anything you have direct control over, and you must be aware of these larger trends. For example, newspaper owners will have been aware that readership is declining across the board. This means that they will have needed to work out, as far as possible, which media in five or ten years' time will be taking up the demand for news and information – whether it may be television, radio or other kinds of publishing. It is no accident that Rupert Murdoch has acquired huge TV interests in Asia, the US and the UK. The big decision on which way to go will affect a whole range of decisions that spin off from it.

• Warning signs

When a business is going well, it is all too easy to relax and assume that you somehow have a golden touch. Be vigilant all the time. Watch your competitors like a hawk; spot what they are doing differently, and ask yourself why. Is it beginning to work for them? Is it affecting your sales? Be aware of anything that could signal a downturn so you can react speedily to correct it. My very first job was for Lesney Products, the manufacturer of Matchbox toys. These were highly successful and amazingly profitable. As far as the management was concerned, the only problems seemed to be how to keep up with demand and how to produce the little Matchbox cars in great enough quantities. Then overnight, or so it seemed, Mattel almost wiped out Matchbox cars by introducing HotWheels, a car that went so much faster that it was the only toy car kids were interested in spending their pocket-money on. If Lesney had thought beyond the short term and been more aware of the volatility of the toy market (which, even in the 1960s, was fickle), or had spotted the advent of HotWheels earlier, they might have been able to change, innovate or develop a better product. As it was, they were left with huge overstocks and enormous problems.

High risk parts of the business

It is not quite accurate to say, as many people do, that all businesses generate 80 per cent of their revenue from 20 per cent of their products, but it is true to say that a relatively small number of products or customers often account for a disproportionately large part of a company's revenue. As leader you must know which these products, services or customers are – as this is where you will be uniquely vulnerable. As a business expands, perhaps because it has followed the fortunes of one big customer, it is crucial to be aware of the key elements which, if the worst happened, would blow you out of the water. If you have two or three key products out of several hundred, watch them closely and monitor trends. Spread your risk as far as possible by developing other products and markets.

Let's look at another example, the soft-drinks producer Schweppes. As managing director it would be clear to you that their main product, tonic, is no longer the popular drink it once was. Sales have been falling for years. It wouldn't take a genius to work out that sales will continue to fall. As managing director, it is your job to co-ordinate a response to this problem. This will lead to a series of questions, such as:

- Can you increase demand for tonic with, for example, an advertising campaign?
- Are there markets for tonic that you have not yet tapped, either in terms of geographical area or consumer profile?
- Can you sell tonic as a mixer for drinks not previously associated with tonic?
- Or do you need a series of new products to take its place?

Answering these questions involves amassing a good deal of detail, but that is not your job; it is up to you to assign research tasks to your subordinates. However, once you have gathered together their research into each option, it is your job to decide which one/s to take. Each one of these avenues would lead to a series of detailed steps that should be followed once you've made your decision, and again these actions would be taken by executives who report to you.

● Diagnosing and dealing with problems

You need excellent management information to alert you to potential problems. Your culture of honesty and openness will help in encouraging people to come to you first, rather than hiding mistakes. The golden rule is: the moment you first suspect that there may be a problem with a member of staff, a product, a part of the service you offer, a geographical area or a department, investigate immediately. Never, never put it off. As in health, small problems left unattended grow into big problems. Tackle it now!

● Strategy

This is the biggie. The biggest big picture issue of them all. This is what they pay you for, and at least half your time should be spent thinking about how to grow the business. I have laid out in Chapter 2 a virtually fail-safe plan for working out what it is you are doing, where you are going in the next few years, and how you are going to get there. Suffice it to say that if you cannot break your addiction to detail long enough to work on this, then you should not be leading your organization.

● Acquisition planning, expansion, going global

Part of your thinking should involve consideration of these issues, each one of which is concerned with growing the business. What are the big moves that will change the future? Are there businesses that you should try to acquire to help you on your way? Are there other markets at home and abroad that you can find your way into?

● Change management

Any new direction involves introducing changes to an organization, and people fear and hate change. The management of change is worth a book in its own right, and is not really something that we were able to deal with in detail in the programmes, busy as we were with fixing current crises in leadership. It was the new leaders who were to face the task of creating and managing the future, and their success would depend on each individual's ability to carry planning, enthusiasm and an understanding of human sensitivities right through the business. It is a truism, but change is the only constant in today's business environment, so the management of this is one of the biggest challenges of being a leader. Successful leaders are the ones who can transform people's perception of change as unwelcome, uncalled for and frightening into a realization that change is essential, much needed, the only way to secure a positive future for everyone – and enormously exciting.

Big picture know-how

You cannot run a business without good information. You need both internal information, reflecting how profitable the business is, and external information, which reflects what is happening in the market and what the competition is up to.

Good financial information is crucial. Being able to understand a set of accounts is crucial. Being able to act on what you see in the accounts is crucial. What I find fascinating is that so many people are uneasy with this kind of information when in fact it is not that difficult – you really can do it. Here are some ways to make it easy for yourself:

1 **Forget the fact that you failed maths at school.**

2 **Understand that there are only three things that really matter:**

> PRICE
> VOLUME
> COST

In other words you can charge more or less for what you are selling; your sales volume will go up or down; and the costs involved in running your business go up and down. Sometimes you can control these three elements; sometimes you cannot. There is nothing abstract about them; they are real.

3 Stop complicating things. Your finance director should produce a balance sheet (showing assets and liabilities) and a profit and loss account (showing income, expenditure and resultant profit or loss) each month. There are many details that (for big picture purposes) are not worth your sweating over. Get your financial people to extract from these figures a set of management accounts that are tailored specifically to your needs. Ask them to lay out the figures in a simple way, so that you can see which is the sales column, which is the costs column, and which is profit. You will need to compare each month's figures against last year's figures and against the budgeted figures. If necessary, you should be able to delve further into the background behind each number. If the numbers are really well presented they should be easy to understand, and things that are unusual should leap out of the page at you.

4 Look for anomalies. Once you understand the accounts, instead of seeing a blur of numbers you will be able to see where the business is underperforming or overspending – what looks high and what looks low. The figures will point to real problems and to real solutions. It goes without saying that you should follow up each anomaly you discover, and find out the details behind the figures. If sales are 20 per cent down, for example, ask the sales director for an explanation, and if necessary break out the figures to find out which salesperson, which product, which customer is responsible for the shortfall. This is the only way to stay on top of the financial performance of the business, to ensure you are meeting your strategic targets, to know what is a mere blip and what is potentially serious, and to deal with problems before they become an emergency.

5 Your staff may also feel frightened and muddled by figures. Make it your business to instil in them an understanding that what they do affects the numbers. Be open with financial information, and use your monthly meetings to go through with your subordinates, line by line, the elements that affect their particular area, so that they are in no doubt about their responsibilities to, and impact on, the bottom line. Make sure they really understand and embrace what you are saying. Too many managers fail to demystify financial information, leaving staff afraid of even looking at it.

Big picture behaviour

● Being a leader

Remember that people look to you as someone who is slightly separate, distant and wise. They want to see in you the qualities of courage, consistency, passion and clarity (see Chapter 1) – and they would be surprised and a little repelled to see you becoming too involved in details of their work. Maintain the distance. Keep your clarity.

● Handling mistakes

You must be big enough to deal with and acknowledge your mistakes. They will inevitably form part of your experience as a leader, and often you will be judged more on your reaction to the things that go wrong than on your successes. Once you have put your hands up, as it were, and admitted fault, the embarrassment is over. It cannot get any worse. What is more, acknowledge jitters; if you suspect you are leading the company headlong down the wrong path, there is more shame in not saying anything at all than in deciding to pull the plug. It is extremely hard to do this, particularly when there is a lot of money at stake, and when the entire company has been working on nothing else for months, but there are times when you simply have to cut your losses. The biggest mistake I have ever made was going into On-Digital at Granada. We had done our homework, we knew that Pay TV was going to be the Next Big Thing, we did not want to be left behind and had laid our plans over a considerable period of time. Our plan was to piggyback with Sky, but at the last minute the ITC, the body governing television, stipulated that Sky was not allowed to be a participant because it already had too dominant a hold on the Pay TV market. Despite my sense that it would be daft to go in without Sky, I felt the momentum was unstoppable and I did not pull out. When I think about this now I am painfully reminded of my first wedding – I suspected it was going to be the biggest mistake of my life, but the church was booked, the gifts had been received, a multitude of minute details had been organized ... and I didn't want to let anyone down. Like many of these cowardly decisions, it caused more pain and grief in the long run.

● See and be seen

When you're not here there are no
clear lines of responsibility
PHIL TO ROBIN, Arrow Ford

We don't notice if the boss isn't here.
If one of the workers isn't here, we notice it
DISGRUNTLED WORKER, County Linen

Part of your job as leader is to be visible. As I have said before, a leader's behaviour is incredibly influential on every layer of an organization, and while I am not advocating a falsely cheery tour of the office every morning, I do believe it is important for you to spread your presence around. It comes back to the sense of security that people need; and a boss who shows interest in and knowledge of what they are doing is immensely motivating. There is another reason for this, which goes beyond the simple internal public relations role. As leader you really need to know exactly who is doing what, you need to pick up any dissatisfaction or negativity in order to nip it in the bud – and you also need to sit down with managers in branch offices in order to be a uniting force. So you should be out of your office almost as much as you are in it. A certain amount of glad-handing at company and client functions is also part of your role – like it or not, you are the public face of your organization, so people will associate your products with you and it is best to relish, rather than resent, this side of your job.

● Networking and deal-making

You should get to know the leaders of the other major businesses in your sector, particularly those who are your major competitors. These contacts are invaluable for learning what is happening in the market-place and may often be the first steps towards deals (mergers, joint ventures, and so on) that could be vital for the future. If you really get to know these leaders you stand a better chance of not being left out and not being taken by surprise when major things happen.

● Making decisions

The capacity to make good decisions quickly is absolutely crucial, and very many organizations lack a process whereby this can happen. At one end of the scale you find companies such as Grand Met, who would respond within days to a proposal: brilliant. At the other is the Civil Service, the aim of which, it seems to me, is never to have to make decisions at all. In between lie the great mass of companies. Many of these tend to stumble towards decisions via a slow and wasteful process of endless form-filling, debate by committee, revisions, counter-revisions and delays.

Of course anything can be debated endlessly, but your aim should be to gather the facts to you need make your decision, and to gather them speedily. If you have not got enough facts, find out whether you can genuinely get hold of more information that will reduce any risk in the decision. Do not use a fact-gathering exercise as a means to postpone a difficult call. In the end you need to rely on the facts you have, plus your instinct and nous. Then you must give a straight yes or no, and move on to the next issue.

I have always been a great believer in the value of the 'decision tree'. You start off with the big decision that has to be made. Stay only with this big decision until you've made it. For example, do we want to move into the German market with our product? If the answer is no, stop talking about it and move on. If the answer is yes, then the next decision is about how. A good starting-point might be: are we going to distribute directly ourselves, or are we going to do it through an agent? If you decide to do it yourself, stop talking about agents and begin discussions about recruitment, location, pricing, and so on. In other words, keep narrowing the issue down, so that you don't just go back again and again to earlier decisions, but really move on to making the decisions that lead to real things happening on the ground.

As an example, let's look at a process involving a difficult decision that needed to be taken while I was at the Arts Council. One of our tasks was to do something about the English National Opera (ENO), which was having a very difficult time and facing possible closure. In no time at all, the Arts Council was discussing details such as the size of the orchestra, chorus numbers, and a whole host of other issues. We went round and round the houses, and we were tackling the problem from the wrong starting-point.

We needed a decision tree approach to sort through the muddle. The first issue to debate was whether we were prepared to let ENO go to the wall. The answer was an unequivocal no. That being so, the second issue was were we happy to back the management team that was currently in charge, or should we insist on a new team? It was agreed that we should back the existing management team. Once that was decided, it was clear that decisions such as chorus size, etc, should be up to them. Each decision had certain consequences, and my job (not an easy one) was to keep everyone on the right branch and stop them harking back to earlier points in the process which had already been agreed upon.

At Granada, we needed to decide whether we were going to get enough growth in the company without an acquisition and, if not, which company we should target. Again there was a pattern of decisions, and each one had to be battled out before moving on to the next. We had 'sweated' the business quite well and we decided that we did need another opportunity to do what we had done with Granada – essentially to take a company with potential but currently underperforming, and knock it into shape. We decided to stick within the hospitality sector in order to complement our existing portfolio. There were three or four companies that were possible contenders, so we needed to work out which one would give the best return. Once we had tested them all and settled on Forte, we had to decide how to go about acquiring it.

The key is not to keep going back. Have all your arguments about each stage, but once you have worked out the route follow the path and don't be deflected, either forwards or backwards. Otherwise you will find yourself going down all sorts of paths and blind alleys, and will foresee all manner of difficulties. Concentrate at all times on the main decision AND NOT THE DETAIL. The detail will follow the decision.

● Getting from thinking ... to doing

As leader, you are the starting-point for the decisions and actions that will build a successful business. Once you have made a decision – really, in your heart of hearts made it – draw up your own action plan. Within minutes you should set a date for the first step, and put it in your diary.

Do sweat some of the small stuff

Of course there are times when small stuff is important:

- All your big picture aims spread a massive amount of detail through the organization. It is certainly not your responsibility to worry about each detail, but you do need to be on top of the people whose concern it actually is, and be sure they are taking care of it.
- Understand the nuts and bolts of your business. Even the best manager cannot go from one industry to another without making it his business to become aware of its workings, as he will be at a loss to know which details are his to worry about and which belong to others. You also need to retain the confidence of your staff, who are entitled to expect you to have at least a broad understanding of what they do.
- Financial details, particularly in relation to meeting targets, are crucial as they tell you whether you are on track or not. The details are different for each business but must be clearly connected with the achievement of the company's larger aims.
- When negotiating, the devil is in the detail. Never go into a negotiation without knowing the details of the consequences of anything you agree to. Otherwise something apparently small may be agreed to, and then turn out to have big implications.

As we saw in Chapter 2, very few of the businesses in the television series had thought about the big issues. Most leaders were operating at what I call the 'paper clips' level. In other words, they were more concerned about having adequate office supplies than where the business would be in five years' time. This is why I set all the key players the task of setting out their objectives for the next few years, thus forcing them to raise their game and address the big picture issues. It was a hard assignment for nearly all of them – the discipline of thinking in this way was completely foreign to them, which was part of the reason why so many of these businesses were floundering. It was no accident that those new managers who were able to see the whole wood, and not just the trees, were the ones who were to succeed.

The **AMT Espresso** brothers had long meetings in which they often beat about the bush, argued about plastic coverings on muffins, and regularly failed to take any meaningful decisions. They all suffered from this clogging of the decision-making process, and seemed unaware that it was the lack of a single decision-maker that was causing the hold-ups as they argued over trivia. Allan was the only one who saw the consequences. He knew that they went round in circles, visiting the same issues over and over again and going nowhere. He showed an intuitive feel for this on the issue of whether or not they should start their own bakery. He knew quite simply that they needed to make a decision and move on. At least then they would not waste further time on something they might not do. There were other organizational problems at AMT that the brothers were aware of, such as the lack of good systems and processes, and they recognized that they needed more information to analyse and understand the business. I felt that Alastair's poor decision-making habits, his tendency to butterfly from issue to issue, and his lack of time management (all small-stuff problems) were going to let him down as a leader, which was why I would have preferred to see the clearer and calmer Allan run the business for a few years.

* * *

At **George Brown & Sons**, the three partners were all stuck doing their old delivery jobs – because they enjoyed getting out and seeing the customers. They were all working terribly hard, believing that if they could just get up a little earlier, just work a little later at night, it would all come good. Quite a few of them had ideas about new directions for the company, although none of the partners had focused on the future at all. When asked to look to the future under their own leadership, most waffled and got easily side-tracked. Only Simon – perhaps with the benefit of being much younger, and having had little hope of ever running the business before I arrived – could clearly see the problems facing the company, the options ahead, and ways of putting them into practice. It was this clarity about the bigger issues that singled him out for the job. He's made a great success of it, too.

* * *

The residents of **Muncaster Castle** were in a bit of a pickle, going round in circles being terribly nice to each other, but all the while not able to think strategically about how to keep the castle from falling into disrepair in the future. Perhaps because there were only four of them, and perhaps because they lived in the castle itself, perhaps because it had been in the family for generations and they rubbed along reasonably well, they all found it hard to step back and see what was really going on. Even the level-headed Iona told me that she wasn't sure I was right about there being nobody in charge – she had a charming way of dodging the key issues. The atmosphere in the castle was emotionally charged with the friction between Iona and her mother, and Iona and her husband, and it was plain to me that unless this could be swept aside with the rest of the castle's accumulated clutter the path to the future would not be clear. One of Phyllida's problems was that she was zooming in on the small details. Instead of seeing the long-term, positive effects of letting part of the castle out to guests, she was stuck, for example, in a worry about them watching her playing cricket on the lawn. As soon as they started to make headway on these sticky issues, Iona and Peter were able to think about the big picture without fear of being scuppered by Phyllida, and map out what they wanted to do.

* * *

Richard Chaplin at **Vernon Road** was right to worry about the detailed marks on fabric – the tears, the stains, the worn patches – but he was approaching the problem from the wrong starting-point. He knew that the business was failing on account of the high volume of returns caused by poor-quality work, and he put this down to poor workmanship and stopped at that. His solution was to focus on the workers and attempt to drive them to greater productivity. Instead, he should have moved several steps back up the cause-and-effect chain and noticed that it was his management style that was causing a lack of motivation, and hence poor-quality work. He seemed to feel angry and to take the difficulties the company was experiencing personally. He could not plan a better approach. He should also have thought bigger when he made the redundancies, and instead of letting a trickle of people go, selling some of the small assets off and then laying off a larger trickle, he should have managed a bigger staff cut-back all at once.

* * *

Sir John Starkey of **Norwood Park** was so absorbed by detail – how the golf course should be laid out, how good each strawberry was – that I knew he would never be able to look at the big picture and work out how to create the £1.5 million or so of income that I believed was needed. His inability to see the future as anything other than an optimistic extension of the present would, in my view, make it more likely that the house and grounds would leave the family before another generation had passed. Henry, for his part, realized that he was getting bogged down in the small stuff ('I have been getting involved in the nitty gritty ... like whether we have got enough tea') but didn't have the management tools to focus on what was important. From their vantage position in the west wing, Suzannah and Johnno seemed to have more of an overall sense of what was going on, and convinced me that they would be much better potential leaders.

* * *

Robin Harris at the **Arrow Ford** dealership was a conundrum. He seemed neither to see the big picture, nor to be a detail man. He was a trader, a dealer, preferring to fly by the seat of his pants or not at all. He had set the business up in the glory days of car dealership, and now that the industry was hitting a low point he was not coping. 'I'm the only one who doesn't do anything. Everyone else has got a job,' he commented mournfully – although this, if he could but see it, is the point. Leaders should not be doing ordinary jobs; they should be leading. Yes, they should make sure there are people to attend to the detail, but their focus should be on the big picture. I must say, though, that a car dealership is a detail business if ever I saw one. It is about making sure that every customer is treated properly, that each part of the business is co-ordinated to deliver the service to the customer. It is ensuring that you do not fail to bill, and get good customer information to ensure proper follow-through. There must be no overstock in the parts department, no mistakes in terms of overbuying on the used cars, and you need to know which cars have been in stock too long. Nigel Bond was, in contrast, much better on detail, and had a better grasp of the business realities in a tough industry. However, worry over details of the deal between Robin and Nigel nearly blew it apart. Both were sticking their heels in over issues that – in the grand scheme of things – were of minor importance in comparison with the overarching need to get the business back on its feet. Eventually we got them to shake hands on the deal, and worry about the minutiae later. I have found that the small haggles often lose a deal. This is daft because most of the niggles can be sorted out after the deal is done.

Alistair Clark, at **The Old Manor Hotel**, was a terrific big picture thinker, and his business was successful as a result. But he was also a workaholic. Inevitably the need to be at work led to an obsession for detail that often got in the way of people's jobs and made them unhappy. He was the kind of man who felt that no one could do their jobs as well as he could, and he meddled with everything. 'He gets involved in things he doesn't have to,' commented one of his sons, in the understatement of the year. This insistence on getting absolutely everything perfect meant that Alistair's way of doing things was so much the norm, so much the only model for a successful business, that no one else was allowed to develop his own capacities and decision-making skills. It was therefore no surprise that his sons were afraid of taking over from him. He was always going to be a hard act to follow. The tragedy was that he desperately wanted them to prove their worth by challenging him to hand over the business to them, but he had failed to develop in them the confidence to enable them to do so. One big thing preventing the sons from carrying out their action plan was the 'small stuff' of their relationship with their father. They were anxious about sticking their necks out, and anxious about taking over the reins from him. As soon as they had managed to see beyond this and grasp the nettle of leadership, the small stuff started to melt away.

CHAPTER SIX

▶ Getting the message across

Stop writing; start talking

Why is it important?

*I don't know what his
plans are*
Jo, Arrow Ford

I have always believed that good communication is one of the keys to successful leadership, both within a company and when dealing with the outside world. The main reason for communicating well is obvious - you have a message to get across to the people who work in your business, which essentially boils down to **What You Are Doing** and **Why You Are Doing It**.

Your people need to understand what you are saying, take it on board, believe in it, and then act in the ways necessary to take the business forward in the direction you want. Leaders who are honest, open and clear in the way they convey information can achieve extraordinary turnarounds. People will start to work together with a renewed sense of purpose, which has a positive effect on their morale and ultimately, of course, on the bottom line. Good communication allows you to share your vision, convey information, and develop good relationships with those around you.

Unfortunately the ability to communicate is something that does not seem to come easily to many leaders, and certainly I met very few people in the course of filming *I'll Show Them Who's Boss* who had even got to first base.

The result was confusion, widespread rumours, diffusion of effort, low morale, and a lack of trust in the management. When I first went into Granada it was in real trouble: its shares were at an all-time low and there was a palpable sense of doom throughout the company. I did not give people a false boost by telling them they were fantastic; I simply gave them very straightforward tasks, and communicated very clearly that we had a one-off chance to sort the business out. In a very short space of time it had become a good place to work in, with a real aura of success.

For everything to survive we've all got
to work together and you've got
to communicate with the other
departments to make it work properly.
The left hand doesn't know what the
right hand is doing
Jo, Arrow Ford

If you asked most people what single thing they would like from their managing director, they would probably say 'more communication'. Fatal! I would be prepared to bet that they are already receiving way too much of it – in the form of documents, memos, reports, briefings, newsletters, press clippings, minutes of meetings, budgets, presentations ... not to mention literally hundreds of e-mails each day, and phone messages on top of that. And I suspect they still feel that they don't really know what's going on! What they need is not more communication, but less communication, and better communication. Remember too that it is a two-way process: as leader, you need your people to communicate with you in order to inform the decisions you will make that will take the business forward.

During the course of writing this I came across so many businesses that were pottering along in a muddle that I came to the conclusion that actually people are often comfortable with not communicating well. Why? Because it protects them from confronting problems head-on, and saves them from having to make difficult decisions. What happens, of course, is that while they are fudging and bluffing and blustering, the wrong people are in the wrong jobs, tasks are being performed below standard, essential action points are not being followed up, opportunities are being lost and the business is going down the tubes. Clear communication is absolutely vital at every level of your business, and if you are one of the people who are happy with muddle, read on. This chapter will get you started on the path to better communication and greater success.

Communicating less

Your job as leader is to wipe out as much of the paper snowstorm as possible and introduce a culture of real, face-to-face communication. The better you are as a communicator, the better you will be as a manager. I take the same basic approach to communicating as I do to all aspects of running a business:

- Be clear: use direct and logical sentences.
- Be consistent: don't give one message today and a different one tomorrow.
- Be simple: remember that you yourself are not that important, much as you might like to appear clever, witty or learned. Long words and complicated sub-clauses hamper effective communication. Aim to get your point over quickly and simply. If in doubt, don't say it – it is far better to say less than to overexplain.
- Be specific: keep in mind what the person receiving your communication needs to know, which is always, without fail, how does this affect me?
- Be visible and approachable, but not too available (a little mystique goes a long way).
- Listen actively to what people say.
- Be friendly, warm and polite even when dealing with difficult issues.
- Use positive body language, open gestures, plenty of eye contact and an upbeat tone of voice.
- If you say that something is going to happen, make sure it really does – when you say it will. If you are not going to deliver, say nothing.
- Don't knock other companies, departments, teams or individuals.
- Don't use 'I'; use 'we'.

- Don't lie.
- Don't blame other people, the markets or the competition. Accept responsibility yourself, show some humility, and move on.
- Don't go around looking gloomy or sulky – it's catching.
- Avoid using bland American positive-thinking speak at all costs. I know I risk being pilloried for this, but I do believe that being over-confident and over-optimistic is not helpful in running a company, however exciting you can make something sound. I have found that people in this country are pretty smart – they do have a sense of irony, and they will see straight through you. Of course you should be positive if things are going well, but if they are not lying about it will not help at all.
- Get the tone right: don't be overly 'matey', but don't be too formal.
- Above all – be yourself. People respond to the humanity in others, and a boss is no different.

These are my general rules. Let's look now at the different ways you might communicate with people: you can speak to a large group, you can talk to an individual face to face, via video conference or on the telephone. Or you can send written reports, memos, letters and e-mails. There is a time and a place for each, but it is vital to get the time and the place absolutely right.

Face to face

If he says can you work overtime
and you say no, he won't talk to you
for two weeks
FACTORY WORKER ABOUT JEFF MASON, Vernon Road

This, above all, is how the majority of your communication with your people should be. It applies particularly to those who report directly to you, but it is also vital for you to be seen as approachable by the wider staff. Face-to-face communication will help you to appear more human. It reduces misunderstandings, and provides greater opportunities for motivation. I have always been suspicious of people who protect themselves with more than one secretary. I have trouble finding enough work for one. The importance of direct communication is true on a personal level too, as I found when I was going through a divorce from my first wife, Maria. It was a very difficult time for both of us, and communicating through lawyers made things worse. The only way to get to the heart of things, speed things up and avoid horrible misunderstandings was to sit down and talk to one another – not easy, but better in the end.

● Meetings

Communication is our downfall,
and I think meetings would
make a big difference
Jo, Arrow Ford (where there were no meetings)

Notwithstanding the above, most meetings are unnecessary. Look carefully at your schedule of meetings and reduce them massively, then do the same for the people who report to you. Have as few as you can, with as few people attending them as possible (no more than eight or ten). The first meeting I chaired at the Arts Council was attended by twenty people: it took nine hours and very little was decided or achieved. So I asked them all to resign and, after a period of time, I reappointed only ten.

You will know whether the reason for the meeting is to disseminate information, to gather information, to plan a campaign or to follow up on agreed action points. Be clear at the start about what the meeting is for – announce it, if necessary – and do not let people veer off the point or get involved in areas that are of no real concern to them. You may find that people allow their personal feelings for or against colleagues to get in the way of clear thinking. Stick to the agenda, keep the detail appropriate to the level of what you are discussing, ensure that someone is taking clear minutes, and never let a meeting go on beyond two hours. People love to sit and chat, but they do lose their concentration and become ineffective after a while. Once, as an experiment, I allowed a board meeting at Granada to go on and on. After a few hours it had careered wildly off track and we were virtually writing story-lines for *Coronation Street*.

● One-on-one meetings

If you try to talk to him, it's
'Shouldn't you be down there working?'
Jo, Arrow Ford

Your monthly meetings with your immediate subordinates are vital. You must come with the minutes of the last meeting, and you must follow up each point. Use these meetings as a chance to convey your passion about the company, motivate your subordinate and keep him or her 'on message'. They will then do this with the people who report to them, and so on down the tiers of management. Ask open-ended questions that lead not to yes or no answers, but ones that point towards an action that needs to be carried out. If you want to know something specific, then ask specific questions. Be wary of hearing what you want to hear, be extremely vigilant and, if you are unclear on a point, go back and check again. If you are communicating clearly with the seven or eight people who report directly to you, they will trust you to tell them the important things. They will know that if there is anything you need to communicate to them, you will do so. This will make them less susceptible to rumours that unnerve them.

If you are having a meeting with someone you do not know very well, take time to establish rapport. The person will have different experiences, different needs and a different 'take' on the world from you, so if you want to be in control of the meeting you must put yourself in his shoes. This is also something to remember when negotiating. Talking face to face also helps humanize you, and can defuse emotionally difficult situations. Remember that there is nothing more humanizing than saying you are sorry. If you apologize for having stuck your heels in, acknowledge the other person's view and say that you need to find the best way through for both of you. You may find they come round to your point of view.

We sometimes start arguing from early in
the morning and go on for the whole day
until we're about ready to collapse
ALLAN, AMT Espresso

● Brainstorming sessions

These are quite different from normal meetings, and certainly have their place. Here the two-hour rule need not apply; indeed, some brainstorming sessions I have led have been spread over the course of a day. It is very useful, as I have said earlier, to get feedback from your staff on general issues to do with the company, the competition, new initiatives, and so on. One way of encouraging communication back to you from the shop floor, as it were, is to hold free-form brainstorming sessions where staff can be open with you about their ideas. Start in a gentle, low-key way, as people tend to take some time to warm up for an exercise like this and you need them to feel comfortable and happy. Eventually you will find ideas coming thick and fast (some brilliant, some awful), so be ready with some coloured pens and a flip chart. These sessions shouldn't be held too often but, when run properly, they will encourage people to feel valued, will promote collective responsibility and will always spark off some great new ideas. Don't bother to hold them if you are not genuine in your search for things that you want to come out of the process. Don't try to be over-organized – a little chaos does no harm at all. If you structure a brainstorming session, you defeat the object of the exercise.

● Question and answer sessions

Hold these occasionally, particularly during a period of change, when you are aware of confusion in the air and small gossipy gatherings of people around the photocopier. There is nothing more damaging to a company than allowing rumours to spread unchecked, so pre-empt this by taking the bull by the horns. Gather people together and allow them to ask any question on any issue that is bothering them, and give open, honest answers unless you are prevented from doing so for legal reasons. The management of change is a difficult thing to accomplish well, but 'demystifying' sessions such as this will help staff to feel involved, consulted and informed. In this way you will work with, rather than against, people; if you use memos, briefing documents or the company newsletter to inform them of complex new situations, you will find that they will form their own ideas of what is happening, sometimes with disastrous consequences.

- ## Annual appraisals

  I hate appraisal systems. They are more often than not completely artificial. The best way of tackling a staff issue is to do it instantly, whether it is to give praise, encouragement or honest, constructive criticism. I can see little point in letting an issue either fester (and get worse) or lie forgotten for months until it is appraisal time. Take the matter up in your next meeting – people need to know now if things are working well or not. Use the annual salary review, if you must, as an opportunity to go over what you have said to someone during the year, and offer pointers and targets for their future development. Remember that nothing should come as a surprise at a review. And if you are giving negative feedback, do so without getting personal.

- ## Conferences and big events

  I enjoy the annual knees-up, and I believe that it plays a really important part in making your staff feel part of an operation that is exciting and going places. It is not for conveying hard information, but a little bit of razzmatazz, a little obvious propaganda, never hurt anyone. Don't stint on the party even if times are tough: a company that cancels its Christmas party gives out the worse possible message. It saves peanuts and takes all the fun out of work.

- ## Giving speeches and presentations

  When presenting decent results or talking about the new directions the business is taking, be upbeat. Make your presentation professional and slick, and hire people to help with equipment, charts, music, visuals – even dancing girls. There are very good mechanisms out there now to support you. Don't worry about being nervous, everybody is (even me). Practise in front of your family – they will give you honest feedback, and if nothing else it will give them a laugh. If you can give your address without notes, great – do it. But if you need to use notes there's no harm provided you don't simply read them out dully. If you can be off the cuff and natural you will appear more real and your passion will come across much more convincingly. Use humour if you can. Taking the mickey out of yourself often breaks the ice. When you have finalized what you want to say rehearse a few times with a friend if you need to, but don't over-rehearse as your delivery can very easily become wooden. Ensure that the flow of thoughts is logical and clear, and that you reinforce key points. Think 'hearts and minds', think about the reactions you want to provoke, and couch your speech in real and compelling terms that the listener can relate to. The old maxim, 'Tell them what you are going to say, say it, then tell them what you have said' is a good one, but I prefer:

1 This is what we are doing
2 This is why we are doing it
3 This is why it is good
4 This is what it means for you

Try **VERY HARD** to keep your presentation to no more than ten minutes – people have a very short attention span. They get bored easily, and, if you bore them, they won't remember what you are saying.

● Announcing bad news

I find that many leaders do well when it comes to spreading the good news, but suddenly clam up when things go wrong, perhaps for fear of scaring people. This is a fatal route to take: let's face it, there is usually widespread knowledge throughout a company that there is something afoot, and the longer you keep news hidden, the lower morale will dip. This is because people will make up their own answers and they will, without fail, be far worse than the reality. Of course, it is never easy to convey news of imminent change, redundancies or cut-backs, but it is possible to be honest, straightforward and open. Work with people rather than against them, tell it like it is, explain exactly where everyone stands, keep focused on the outcomes, and you will be able to move on in a positive manner. If you have made a mistake, admit it – people respond well to leaders who admit failures, accept publicly that they made bad decisions, and apologize. There will sometimes be legal constraints on what you can and cannot say, but do above all avoid what I call company-speak – people will see right through you. See also chapter 4 on the dos and don'ts of redundancy planning.

● Phone calls

> *I never allow a phone system*
> *that comes in to a switchboard.*
> *I always speak to the person*
> NIGEL, Arrow Ford

I hate the phone – you cannot see people's reactions, facial expressions and body language, so you are only receiving part of the message. It is not uncommon to find that your notes of a phone conversation do not tally with those of the person you were speaking to. Use it only for brief conversations on day-to-day matters. If humanly possible, never use the phone to convey messages that are likely to have a serious impact on the recipient.

● Video conferencing

This can be useful for communicating with overseas staff, but don't use it just for the sake of it. There is something deeply unreal about talking to a screen and being talked to by someone on a screen – it always makes me feel as if I'm on the set of *Star Trek*. If at all possible, get your people round the table.

Writing it down

> *I write it down yet still it*
> *is not being done*
> RICHARD, Vernon Road

● Formal documents

Even if you are not presenting them live, the basic rules for effective speech – writing apply to written strategies, plans, proposals – whatever you like to call them – anything, basically, that puts forward your ideas for the future development of your department or the company. You may have spent months working on your plans, but don't be tempted to make the resulting document into something grand and important. Write as you would talk, in succinct, clear language, cutting out jargon, with logical sentences, short paragraphs and bullet points. You don't need to repeat points as often as you do when you are talking, but make sure that each step is clearly outlined and don't jump to conclusions; everything must make sense in a logical sequence. If you are selling an idea or a product, couch it in real and compelling terms that would appeal to you if you were the recipient. This will make it easier for people to agree to what you are proposing. If you are writing a report, remember to include an 'executive summary' and emphasize your conclusion. If you can, deliver documents in person – the impact will be much greater.

I once received a strategy document for a company I had just joined that was as thick as a doorstep: my heart sank just looking at it. The next year I had cut it down to eight pages, and things started looking up.

Letters and faxes

Come on, no one writes letters these days unless it is to their Great-aunt Agatha (and she'll probably reply by e-mail). Faxes and e-mail are more immediate. Faxes are particularly useful for documents that require a signature, to show amendments to a document or for documents that for whatever reason cannot easily be e-mailed. When writing anything, be aware that it can be misinterpreted.

E-mail

Be afraid; be very afraid. E-mails are out of control. Many people receive hundreds of these little messages each day, few of which do anything other than cover someone's backside. The dry, truncated nature of e-mails means that they are also very open to misinterpretation. I am sure we are all aware of the advantages of e-mails, but do think very carefully before you hit the 'reply all staff' button, or 'blind copy to' button – you don't have to tell everyone everything, and they don't need to know everything. The problem is that it is so addictive. We are all responsible for this terrible, insidious boom in useless information. You have to distinguish between really communicating, and simply dumping data. I agree with Michael Eisner, the chairman of Walt Disney, who said, 'I have come to believe that if anything will bring about the downfall of a company or maybe a country, it is blind copies and e-mails that should never have been sent.' Some companies, such as Phones4U, in a brave attempt to halt this waste of time and money, have even banned internal e-mailing. Do the same in your company if you dare!

If people receive daily e-mails and memos from you, their leader, they will start to ignore them. It is much better, if possible, to walk around to someone's office and talk to them directly. Your people should know that when they receive a written communication from you it really means something.

SMS texting

An increasingly popular method of communicating with colleagues, this is another incredibly useful tool, but is also a potentially disastrous source of misunderstandings. The friendliest of messages can sound abrupt and rude, so use with care. I recall that one company recently sacked hundreds of employees, and informed them by text. Hardly an object lesson in good staff relations.

Company newsletters

Please, scrap the newsletter – it is costly, and nobody reads it. Be honest, don't you cringe when you read them, with their false chumminess, blandly optimistic messages from the chairman, salesmen of the month, and Sharon in accounts' new baby (it's far more exciting if Sharon brings the baby in to show it around). People always see through this kind of banal propaganda. They are much smarter than you think. Newsletters are also not going to unite a company – people out in the field have an inherent distrust of head office, and those in head office think that everyone else is less important than them. No one is really interested in the information in newsletters – they are a glossy waste of money. Related, but with the potential to be more useful, is the company intranet, a virtual notice-board. If it can be used by staff to access genuinely useful up-to-the-minute information, such as background details on clients, product specifications, new products, process changes and so on, then it's worth having. If it doesn't do this, get rid of it, because if it is out of date even by a day or two people will start to ignore it.

All the above are specific opportunities for conveying your message correctly and effectively. Never forget, however, that communication is a daily exchange of messages about what the business is doing, where it is going and how it is getting there. It is also about communicating with the outside world.

External communication

There are three areas you need to get absolutely right. Branding, press relations and your website.

● Branding

You must above all be consistent. We are bombarded with thousands of advertising stimuli every day, so for your message to get across in this crowded world you must say the same thing over and over and over again. No matter how simple your message (the Avis slogan 'We try harder' is a brilliant example), keep on saying it. Whether you want to sell the best coffee in the UK, be the finest fruit and vegetable supplier in the West, have the best hotel in Fife or the cleanest laundry in Essex, repeat your message *ad nauseam*. You may well get bored with it, but do not tire of it and do not change it. This goes for your logo and your marketing material: everything that leaves your office must convey a slick, consistent message.

● Press coverage

I am always surprised by how little impact press coverage has on 'hard' aspects of a company such as sales or stock-market price, and how much it has on staff morale. If positive things are being said about the company they work for, staff feel proud and happy to work there. Conversely, negative press comments make people feel low; worse still, their friends and family begin to pretend that they feel sorry for them. Very quickly your staff are embarrassed to admit where they work, and soon they will be looking for another job. As chief executive, you must do everything possible to ensure positive press coverage: always be available to talk to journalists. Use PR (public relations) advisers if your business is large enough – they are useful sources of information on which publications do what, and can place articles for you – but don't use them as a way of avoiding talking to the press. Return calls to journalists, don't be frightened, be friendly and helpful, and be frank about areas you cannot discuss for legal reasons. It is true that journalists are often looking for a particular angle to make a good story, and that good angle may often be one that gives a negative spin to your business, but I have found that the best policy is to ask them exactly what information they are after and – if possible – give it to them. It has always worked for me, with one notable exception, when a journalist published an inaccurate piece about AMT Espresso, who were at that time threatening to sue the BBC for allegedly making them look 'incompetent'. I spent a great deal of time going through the facts with him yet when the story was printed I felt it veered well away from the truth.

● Website

Make sure you have one. Make sure it is brilliant. Use experts to make it look professional, attractive, bang up to date, and usable. Two warnings: it is useless if potential customers cannot find it via search engines like Yahoo or Google; likewise if, once they have found your site, they cannot place orders (depending, obviously, on the kind of business you are).

Let there be confusion

*It's not a very pleasant
atmosphere to work in*
LORRAINE, George Brown & Sons (during selection process)

Yes, really! I know I have argued for clarity and simplicity of communication throughout this chapter, but muddle and confusion do in fact have their place. Indeed, it can be counterproductive to seek clarity at a time when things really are confused. As a new leader, or at times when you need to reassess where the company is at, and where it is going, you must expect a period of confusion. Part of the process you will go through is a systematic gathering of information, and part of this will of course involve effective communication with your staff to garner ideas on possible future directions. It will be particularly complicated if the business has hit a tough patch and you are not entirely sure where the answers lie. What will come out of this process is a bundle of confused thoughts – people may be in two minds about something; it is not uncommon to see several possibilities, each of which has its own merits, and new 'ingredients' that alter everything often enter the melting-pot at a late stage. If you bring this period to an end prematurely you will not have all the information you need to move on effectively. You must allow enough time for all the conflicting ideas to be thrown up in the air, and find out where people who are crucial to the business are coming from (as opposed to where you think they are), and then it is up to you to unravel the mess in order to arrive at your clear answer. Look at what happened every time I arrived at a business for *I'll Show Them Who's Boss* and started to stir things up. Without fail, issues came up that upset and disturbed almost everyone – but eventually we came through this unsettling period of confusion and arrived at a crisp view of what should happen to ensure a successful future. If you are newly in charge of a business, use your precious objectivity, which will be very short-lived, to cut through the muddle.

We've been plodding along without
really knowing there's an emotional
crisis actually happening
MICHAEL CLARK, The Old Manor Hotel

Communication was invariably going awry in *I'll Show Them Who's Boss*. In some cases it was part of the general muddle; in others it was causing catastrophic problems.

At **Vernon Road** Richard and Henry Chaplin were desperate to turn the company into a profitable concern, but low productivity and poor quality of work were threatening to wipe out profits. There was a terrible atmosphere on the factory floor: rumours were rife, workers were suspicious and feared that the owners wanted to 'level the place and sell it to a developer'. Richard claimed that he had been trying to increase sales by selling fabric to the high street fashion industry and had even increased staffing levels to cope with the orders. Despite the increased orders, the workers were hanging around drinking tea and not concentrating on their work. Jeff Mason, the shop-floor manager, tried to push them into efficiency. Richard thought his staff were responsible for the lack of motivation, totally failing to see that the fault lay with his poor management.

I believed that the biggest single thing the owners had to do for the business to be successful was to make the people on the shop floor feel enthusiastic about it. I advised Richard to gather them together and just talk to them about his fears, concerns and hopes for the company. I suggested he should explain that he genuinely wanted to build the business, and try to come across as a sympathetic human being. He seemed to accept this: 'I've asked the guys in here to do a lot of changing, so perhaps it's down to me to do a bit of changing as well.' He called the workers in for a meeting. One of them told him how happy and excited they were when he bought the business, until they felt that he was starting to blame them for the company's woes. Richard admitted he was wrong, and explained that he had been facing major crises every day from the moment he started. 'But why didn't you talk to people about that?' someone asked. His response? 'I didn't have time.' Wrong! There should always be time for something as vital as helping staff understand what it is that management is trying to do.

However, there were many positives about this speech. He publicly admitted that he had made mistakes, he explained how management and work-force stand and fall together, and he promised to talk to the staff as often as was necessary. 'I just need to be given a second chance,' he begged. I was impressed at his willingness to humble himself, and I felt there was a chance that he might be able to move some way towards being the kind of boss who listens and communicates instead of erecting barriers between himself and the staff. Kevan, one of the shop-floor workers, summed it up with amazing managerial insight: 'When everybody's a team and everybody's happy he'll get bigger profits. Until then we'll see.'

He was right to be sceptical. Before long, Richard was back to his old ways – being unavailable, stomping around looking like thunder, and failing to communicate honestly and openly. The company continued to suffer from returns and debts, and Richard eventually realized that he needed to make staff cut-backs. This naturally created a lot of bad feeling, and it was up to management to reassure the remaining workers that their jobs were safe, while at the same time persuading them to work even harder (see Chapter 4 for more on redundancy). Richard then thought it was a good idea to send the unpopular Jeff on to the shop floor with a badly worded letter that supposedly explained what had happened and attempted to rally the troops for renewed efforts to save the business. Here is an extract:

Since the early part of this year the company has been performing well with a month on month break-even, or small profits being reported. However, June was a disastrous month. It is extremely important for the future of the business and its employees that the company grows and remains profitable. Yesterday saw the start of a new structure to be introduced which unfortunately meant the redundancy of twelve people. No further redundancies are planned as long as we continue to meet the expected operating levels.

This is dreadful. It is negative, gives very little information, and fails to encourage the remaining staff. Worse, it ends with a threat. I watched Jeff take this message around the shop floor and could see on the workers' faces how much they mistrusted him. This could have been a wonderful opportunity, but it was wasted, and the letter did more harm than good. Jeff, however, reported to Richard that the staff accepted and understood the news. It was time for Jeff to go, and I told Richard this in no uncertain terms.

This led to another extraordinarily convincing piece of oratory by Richard (see page 102–3), in which he praised his staff, empathized with the difficulties they had been going through, promised them that there would be no more redundancies and explained why he had let Jeff Mason go.

I was impressed once again with Richard's ability to speak from the heart – it was passionate, it was convincing. I had the sense that there was a real possibility of a new beginning here. But a week later Jeff was back, with few words of explanation. For once I was speechless – I had never seen anything so stupid done in management terms in my life. The workers were shocked (but, maybe, not surprised) that Richard could so easily go back on his word. This disastrous U-turn proved to me that Richard's skills did not lie in management.

The film provided an object lesson in how not to communicate, which is why I have quoted from it so extensively in this book. In my opinion, Richard broke so many of the rules – he seemed bad-tempered, remote, shied away from open communication and allowed his financial concerns to spill over into criticisms of his work-force. If he really had sufficient orders coming in to save the business, he could have solved all his problems by being consistent, open, honest, down-to-earth and friendly – the sort of boss people want to work hard for.

* * *

Each of the other family businesses we looked at had difficulties with communication. Many of the problems, it is true, came down to the fact that those involved were all related and had brought suitcases full of emotional baggage into their businesses (I will talk more about family issues in Chapter 7). As an outsider, I was able to form clear views of where communication was breaking down, and the people concerned (usually!) felt relieved to have someone who could get them talking, help them clarify the issues and resolve the problems that were preventing them from moving forward. If you can stand back in an emotionally detached way, and break down the problems so that you see them as an outsider would see them, you should find that you can identify your own communication difficulties.

At **George Brown & Sons** the family had never faced up to what was going wrong in the business, bumbling along in their old ways, working their fingers to the bone, liked by all but losing money. There were no systems for effective communication and their company was in a mess. When I arrived they were reluctant to go through that uncomfortable period of confusion while we sorted the business out, and as a result they made a terrible decision. The three senior partners held a secret meeting – breaking the very important rule of openness – and appointed Paul, the eldest, as managing director even before I had had a chance to talk to each member of the family in turn to assess their capabilities. They were in such a hurry to get out of the uncomfortable period of muddle and avoid any 'nastiness' that they took the easy (and therefore worst) option. Willingness to acknowledge what is happening is a very good test of a company's strength – and at that point communication at George Brown & Sons was very poor. There was a marked contrast as soon as Simon took charge. His approach is to deal directly with people, rather than writing memos; he confronts problems head-on and has instilled a culture of openness in the company.

* * *

At **The Old Manor Hotel**, in Fife, the Clark family also had some major communication problems. Alistair, the domineering father, admitted he was a bully ('Someone yesterday called me a Rottweiler,' he once said, a little proudly). He was brusque and didn't baulk at swearing at staff, believing that one of the jobs of a boss was to be, well, bossy. Although he could be very direct and clear in the way he communicated, it was his manner that was frightening. I really don't think he understood just how frightening he was to deal with. He terrified those who worked for him and came across as a very cold person, something that always rings alarm bells in people, including me. The key problem I saw, though, was the chronic lack of communication between him and his two sons Michael and George, who would eventually inherit the business. Alistair had not been clear about what he really wanted to do: whether it was to retire altogether, stay on as chairman/mentor, keep going, or sell up completely. He had been reluctant to commit himself to a decision because he had concerns about what his sons might do with the business once they got their hands on it. They in turn would not say what they would do, because they were unsure of the role their father wanted to play, and were unsure anyway about what they wanted to do. Catch-22! As a result they were all going round in circles. There was a great deal of anger and frustration that had not been acknowledged or dealt with. What they needed was the courage and clarity to sit down and hammer out what the issues really were. When we did eventually get them to sit down some very interesting admissions emerged. George and Michael confessed that they did want their father involved in the business, and Alistair admitted that he did not want to retire, but that his awareness of some of their weaknesses made him reluctant to give up control. Alistair was more honest than we gave him credit for. He really did want to know where the boys were coming from and whether they were committed enough to the business. However, he himself was never sure what he really felt, and tying down what all three of them really wanted to do was a painstaking process.

Eventually it was Michael and George's strategic plan (see Chapter 2) that turned around Alistair's view of his sons, and started to open up the possibility that he could trust them to take over. I was surprised and gratified to see that he softened a little during the course of making the programme. He tried very hard to take on board what was being said to him and to learn that he needed to praise more and use anger less. By the time I left I was truly optimistic that he would take my advice, and give his sons support and praise as they carried out their plans for the business and encourage them even when things went wrong.

* * *

There was a terrible clash of communication styles at **AMT Espresso**. Alastair McCallum-Toppin was sometimes arrogant and not always clear in his thinking – a definite over-communicator, if ever I met one; Allan was sound and sensible but shy; and Angus sometimes seemed confrontational and stubborn. It was a long time since they had sat down together as a family and talked about anything unrelated to the business; it seemed to me that they often related to each other as opposing warriors rather than as human beings – said Alastair to Angus: 'You say, "We do this and we do that, we fight and we do this, and we both think the same and we have the same experience, and this and this and that" – and I totally disagree. I totally, totally and utterly disagree. We're completely different people, we don't even look alike. We have different mentalities, we have different experiences, we have different attitudes, we have different hobbies. We're totally different, yeah? The only thing that ties us together is that we're brothers by name.' When Alastair was late for meetings with me., he never communicated that he was going to be late and never explained why he was or apologized. This is not acceptable behaviour in a leader. It shows total disregard for those who work for or with him. It also shows an inability to organize himself. I felt that Allan would be the steadiest leader, and the fact that he was the one who dealt with the company's many hundreds of staff perhaps pointed to the fact that his communication skills were the best of the bunch.

* * *

Communication was a real problem at **County Linen**, and much of the trust between management and staff had broken down owing to a series of promises that were not fulfilled. Anthony rarely held meetings with his floor managers, but I started to realize that this unwillingness to communicate - a shyness, almost - was a family trait. I felt that none of the family members dealt frankly with the others. When Dudley decided to organize his own meetings with the managers - which might have undermined Anthony's confidence in himself and the workers' confidence in Anthony - Dudley simply brushed it aside, claiming he could see no harm in it. Anthony was obviously upset, but was unable or unwilling to confront his father and voice his deep sense of hurt. There was never going to be a clear and open discussion of all the issues at stake when fundamental communication problems such as this could not be solved.

* * *

Iona at **Muncaster Castle** was a pretty good communicator. She had a nice relationship with the staff, who liked her and worked hard for her. She was determined, could think clearly, had a good sense of humour and was able to laugh at herself, although I detected a tendency to duck difficult issues. When asked by her husband what the family should do, her answer was 'Not fight'. The biggest issue she faced was one of trust - between her and her mother: Phyllida was uneasy about handing over power, and was reluctant to give up her involvement in the running of the castle. She feared that Iona would set up new developments without informing or consulting her. There were some potential new ventures, such as turning part of the castle into holiday lets, that had not been discussed in full because of Phyllida's angatonism towards the idea. I was also concerned about Iona's communication with her husband Peter, which was often poor, perhaps because of the time taken up in running the castle together. They needed to open up better channels of communication, stop sniping at each other, and operate much more as a team. Even their son recognized that they needed to 'speak to each other without arguing'. Iona's non-verbal communication was amazing: she could torpedo an idea by a twitch of an eyebrow. This form of communication is dangerous because it doesn't allow for a reply - it is one way only. The key to fostering more trust in a relationship is, as we have seen, clear communication. Once Iona realized that this was the stumbling-block, she and Peter were able to present a united front and explain her plans for the future coherently to her parents. Her mother in particular - rather like Alistair in Fife - needed to be convinced that the castle and estate were in good hands and were going to be well looked after for the coming generation. It was also clear that Iona would need to continue to keep her mother informed of what was happening in order to keep family relations sweet.

* * *

Robin Harris at **Arrow Ford** was a master of the art of avoiding communication. I am about as anti-meetings as you can get, but Robin held hardly any meetings, and a leader must have some vehicle to convey information and discuss results. At Arrow Ford no one knew what was going on, people were not motivated, and nothing was being followed up. 'The staff don't always know what's expected. It's got to be from the top down,' said daughter Sam. There was such a lack of communication in the company that when Robin eventually allowed us to see the financial records, his accountant almost went into shock. Luckily, Nigel Bond had great people skills: he understood about the importance of face-to-face communication and openness. He gave a much-needed speech to the staff on taking over as managing director which wasn't so much rousing as friendly, open and positive. The impact was immediate – all the staff were delighted. And it may have been politically astute of him to say to Robin's daughters, 'I can't do it without you', but I'm sure it was genuinely meant.

HOW EFFECTIVE A COMMUNICATOR ARE YOU?

We all have our own personal styles of conveying what it is we think, feel or want. Give yourself a score from 0 to 4 in the space beside each question, where 0 = not the case, 1 = hardly ever the case, 2 = sometimes the case, 3 = often the case, 4 = usually or always the case. Add up your total when you have completed the exercise. Be honest in your answers, otherwise you will be wasting your time.

I express my ideas logically and clearly when I speak ☐
I express my ideas logically and clearly when I write ☐
I deal with people face to face rather than on paper ☐
I have no more than two meetings per week ☐

I think about what I am going to say before I say it ☐
I enjoy dealing with the people in my business ☐
I am open and honest ☐
I stick to what I say I will do ☐
I do not have any secrets from the people who report to me ☐
I am not afraid of dealing with emotional people ☐
People like me ☐
People respect me ☐
I give praise and encouragement freely ☐
I am willing to apologize whether I have made a mistake or not ☐
I am able to put myself in someone else's shoes ☐
I do not lie ☐
I behave in the same way at work as I do at home ☐
I deal with problems as and when they arise ☐
My meetings last for no more than two hours ☐
I am able to clarify muddle ☐

If your total score is in the 0–40 range, you are probably experiencing difficulties in relating to people. Take a long hard look at the way you communicate with people and pinpoint areas that you can improve. Even if you are not leading a business, the ability to communicate well is an essential life skill.

If your total score falls between 41 and 65, you are showing potential and need to work on the areas where you have scored the lowest. If you are running a business you will be experiencing some problems and should certainly read this chapter again and take real steps to address areas of weakness. Chapter 3, which covers dealing with people, should be of help to you.

A total score between 66 and 80 shows that you are already communicating well. Be vigilant, because problems arise very easily if even one piece of communication misfires. Keep in mind my maxim: if you can't say it well, don't say anything at all.

CHAPTER SEVEN

▶ Blood is thicker than water

Family businesses are like family weddings – and we all know how difficult they can be

The heart of the matter

One of the unique aspects of *I'll Show Them Who's Boss* was the fact that the series focused on family-run businesses. While they shared common problems of leadership and management with non-family businesses – and this book has so far looked at the lessons that can be learnt from their failings – there were particular issues and problems that raised their heads each time, and these were specific to family businesses. One of the biggest problems with a family-run company is that it is a respectable vehicle for bringing raw, destructive emotions to the surface – angst that often has nothing to do with the business and everything to do with relationships. The danger with these companies is that they may fail because family issues cloud business issues, and there is no easy mechanism to enable the most talented members to come through and lead.

We are family

There are lots of good reasons for starting up a business with members of your family. Traditionally, family members are prepared to work harder, putting in longer hours for less pay. There is a sense of teamwork, of all pulling in the same direction, all profits going back to a strong unit of people who all fundamentally care about each other. There is a great drive to make the thing work, and a personal pride in making it successful. Customers tend to like buying from a family business because they like the idea of the personal touch. There is a feeling that you will be treated better, that you might get a better price, that you are dealing with real people, and that perhaps this business is not as commercial and hard-nosed as other ones.

I was amazed to discover that as many as 70 per cent of UK companies are actually family-owned. Part of the reason for the size of this figure, I suspect, is the number of immigrant families who find that running their own business is the only way to survive in a new country where there are difficulties in breaking into other institutions. Asian, Jewish, Chinese and eastern European people in particular are highly entrepreneurial and family-orientated.

Despite the very real positive aspects to family businesses, I'm afraid there can be many negative ones too, and the more I delved into the background behind the business problems, the more apparent they became. I am not a psychologist or a therapist – although that was what was sometimes needed during the making of these films. I do, however, have a deep interest in what makes people tick, because all businesses are fundamentally about the people.

Emotional baggage

The shared history, and the fact that family members have often grown up together, means there are strong emotions, entrenched ways of behaving, established hierarchies, ancient enmities and opposing factions. I have never found as much anger, mistrust, hurt and resentment as that between the relatives working in the businesses in the series, although of course there was a great deal of care and affection as well. In terms of the business issues themselves, it was easy for me to see what should be done. What had been happening in every case was that commercial decisions were muddied by emotional baggage. There was huge lack of clarity, and very few of the companies were being run in anything approaching a professional manner. As it turned out, my role was as much to try to loosen the psychological blockages as it was to dispense business advice. The business advice was always the easiest part.

So, while family businesses start from a position of enormous strength, their very nature can cause fault lines in their structure. These fault lines become acutely apparent when the time comes for a business to be handed over from one management team to another – on from one generation to the next. In this chapter I will offer my views of how things can go wrong when businesses are run by people who are related by blood or marriage, and I will point to where possible solutions may lie.

● The games people play

There is a branch of psychology called transactional analysis (TA), which I am reluctant to give too much weight to, but which I think is interesting in the context of family businesses. TA is to do with how people function in their everyday relationships, and what their behaviour says about their personality. According to TA, there are three different 'ego-states': the adult, the parent and the child. The idea is that at times we behave like one of our parents; at others we revert to behaving as we did when we were a child, and sometimes we behave like a responsible grown-up. When we feel insecure, frightened, angry or under stress we revert to parent or child states. I surmise from this that, if we are under stress as adults and dealing with our real parents or children, as indeed people often are in family businesses, then our behaviour is all the more polarized and damaging in a business context.

● Over-reacting to criticism

In a non-family business environment, if a worker is criticized by his boss he may take it on the chin at the time, then go home and sound off to his spouse or partner. In a family business there is the freedom to express emotion that is acceptable at home, but the danger is that this is potentially explosive at work. At George Brown & Sons, where there are as many as eighteen members of one family, this had really clogged up the decision-making process. 'I don't like criticism of my son and I'm sure my partners don't like criticism of their children, and they also like decision-making. So you get a split decision all the time,' said David.

● Misplaced loyalty

Richard Chaplin worked his way up in his father Henry's previous business before buying Vernon Road. Although Richard had been promoted to managing director at the previous company, I always suspected that Henry knew deep down that Richard was not right for the job. When I asked if he had ever praised him, he said he felt Richard hadn't done a good job – yet. I wondered how long he had been unable to tell a few home truths to his son. Their colleague Jeff Mason, who was so unpopular with the work-force, was almost like a family member to Henry and Richard: they had worked with him for the past twenty-odd years. So although they initially followed my advice to let him go, their strong friendship with him overcame their business sense, and a week later he was back, to the surprise and irritation of some of the workers.

Sir John Starkey's faith in his son Henry's ability to take on the management of Norwood Park was touching but totally unrealistic. He sometimes committed the cardinal sin of seeing only what he wished to see – the future fourth baronet of Norwood Park – and ignored the facts that were plain to me and, indeed, to some who worked for him. I wasn't altogether surprised, but in a sense it was astonishing that he appeared to cling to the old tradition of primogeniture despite having three bright and able daughters, any of whom would probably have made a better fist of the job than Henry.

Dudley Moore at County Linen also found it hard to accept that one of his sons simply wasn't up to the job. We quite rightly regard loyalty as a positive characteristic, but misplaced loyalty is often simply cowardly and paralyses progress. The fact that all these people were related made what should have been a simple process incredibly complicated and sensitive.

● It's a hard world

You're not women;
you're my daughters
ROBIN, Arrow Ford

Sometimes – less often in my experience – the opposite happens, with parents denying perfectly competent offspring the chance to progress in the business. In a misguided fatherly attempt to show them that the world didn't owe them a living, Robin was holding back his two daughters from real involvement in the business. Sam and Jo both worked for Arrow Ford, but were not in management positions and were not aware of the grave financial situation. They were both capable and talented, and had asked their father for more responsibility, but each had been passed over for promotion and thwarted at every turn. 'I don't want the staff thinking my daughters are mollycoddled – I want them to realize that they earn their money and they're not just here for the ride.' Ironically, if they had not been related to Robin they might have been promoted sooner. I wonder if sometimes we are not hardest on those we love the most. I hoped that under Nigel's management Sam and Jo would be given solid training, more opportunities, more involvement, and a chance to see if they could genuinely help run the business. The more able – but just as obstinate as Robin – Alistair Clark in Fife clung to power, treating his middle-aged sons as children. The ability to lead is inherent, but unless children with potential are given a real chance to do it no one will ever know if they actually can.

● Unspoken issues

Without this antagonism between
us we wouldn't be so energetic
GEORGE CLARK, The Old Manor Hotel

All families are dysfunctional in their own ways, I suppose, and one side-effect of people knowing each other very well is the view that, somehow, some things do not need to be said. In some cases, there are scars that run so deep that things simply cannot be discussed openly. In others, things are left unsaid because of the risk of rocking the boat or upsetting a family member. Family businesses often know of other family businesses, and other people's disasters haunt them. They are all able to cite instances of children gambling the profits away, of them expanding too fast, of them destroying the very nature of the business. Phyllida, the matriarch of Muncaster Castle, was terrified of handing over to her daughter in case she herself was turfed out on to the street with nowhere to go. Both she and Iona were indirect communicators, preferring to express disapproval by a frown rather than in open discussion. This was clearly something of a family trait, but one that thwarted decision-making. Robin and his daughters were stuck in a terrible inability to be frank with one another – the girls avoiding their depressed father; the father unaware of the emotional scars of their childhood, and unable to deal with the impact of his own troubled personal life on the business. I so wanted him to spend more time with Jo and Sam: I knew they would welcome him in if only he could bring himself to come out of his shell. In Fife the sons, George and Michael, had been anxiously waiting for their father Alistair to decide if and when he was going to hand over the business to them. Meanwhile, Alistair was waiting to find out what his sons wanted to do with it if they had the chance ... and all the while nothing was happening and everyone was frustrated. One of the major unspoken issues in family businesses is who is going to take over, and when. The reason it is not discussed openly is for fear of causing upset and distress.

Other things that are brushed under the carpet and allowed to fester are old wounds and ancient injustices that have been allowed to encroach upon office life. Alastair, the youngest AMT Espresso brother, was resentful of Angus, who had been born at a point in their parents lives when there was a great deal of money around: he was 'born with a silver spoon in his mouth'. By the time Alastair was born his father had lost his fortune, times were hard, and the boy grew up with an inbuilt sense of inequality. Meanwhile I felt that Suzannah at Norwood Park held back in her eagerness to get her hands on the estate, not actually coming out and being clear about what she wanted. Of course, we can all understand the very human reasons for this, but the result was a subtle but very definite battle going on between her and her younger sibling Henry.

• Fights, feuds and sibling rivalry

We are like two rams on a
mountain top
ANGUS, AMT Espresso

The only real contenders for the leading role at George Brown & Sons were not necessarily siblings but were of the same generation, and old issues came creeping out. I was told at one point that Simon couldn't possibly get the job because he once nearly set fire to someone at a party! (Not quite true, I was told, more a trick that went awry.) When I listened to the three McCallum-Toppin brothers at AMT Espresso arguing over the colour of coffee cups, or whether to bring in Kit-Kats or Belgian chocolates, it was clear to me that they had been fighting over their teddies since they were small boys. The fact that they were now running a multimillion-pound business made absolutely no difference – the stakes were higher, but they were still at loggerheads. They simply couldn't rise above the nature of their relationship.

I sensed a degree of enmity between the Starkey children, and rivalry over who would get to live in the house: would it be the son, who was due to inherit, or would it be someone better able to run the estate? Underneath a really charming veneer there was often a glance of anger and fierceness that was quite frightening. Meanwhile in Fife, Alistair almost wanted his sons to fight him for the business, in order to prove that they really wanted it (which may be no bad thing, as I will explain later).

● Established hierarchies

When I mentioned Simon being the boss it was like I Claudius – *murder the mother and do the brother in!*
DAVID BROWN, George Brown & Sons

From delivery boy to boss all in one fell swoop? It just shouldn't work like that should it?
RUTH, George Brown & Sons

Families have their own hierarchies and reporting structures which can not only cut across a business hierarchy, but are often diametrically opposed to what is right for the company. The Browns were very unsettled by my suggestion that anyone who wanted the top job could apply for it. 'We are both in our fifties and it is only right that one of us should be in charge,' said David of himself and Paul. It upset the idea of the family's accepted structure and set sibling against sibling, daughter against father, cousin against cousin. Lorraine, one of the daughters, spoke of her initial horror: 'It never crossed my mind that I could be dad's boss. I wouldn't dream of stepping over them and saying, "I can run your business better than you can."' What I was doing was trying to overcome the 'I'm there because I'm daddy's son' element of family businesses and bring in a meritocracy where the best person for the job would get it. This went down so badly with a few of the older members that they had an unscheduled meeting and decided to appoint one of the owners, Paul, as the new managing director. This stunned me – he was certainly not my first choice for leader, but I could see that this was the easiest and least threatening decision. I had to do some fast pedalling in order to get them to reconsider my plan to hear everyone out separately, and to allow me to decide who would be the best candidate. In the ordinary way of things a bright young man like Simon should have been spotted and given challenging jobs to bring him on; in a family business everything militates against this – as a second cousin he would have had no hope of ascending the throne.

At Muncaster Castle the family operated in a very traditional manner, as is the way of old English families. Everyone deferred to the grandmother outwardly, and allowed her to have her say, but resentments were bubbling underneath. There was a very genteel, but very strong, power struggle going on – and there was potentially a huge rift opening up between the generations. In the Starkeys' case choosing Henry rather than overturning the family edifice would have been the easy choice. The reality was that this edifice was much more fragile than Sir John realized. Suzannah, the big sister, was fond of her younger sibling Henry but, quite naturally, resentful of the fact that he would get to own and run the wonderful estate despite the fact that she was older, and in a better position to run it well. In retrospect it is absolutely clear that when I advised Sir John to hand Norwood Park over to her instead, he simply couldn't contemplate it.

In a business where there is a mix of family and non-family, there is additional potential for trouble. Family members can abuse their favoured position, and non-family members may not know quite where they stand *vis-*

à-vis the family. This can be divisive and harmful, and if not handled well can lead to communication and decision-making problems.

● The all-powerful father figure

I see my dad as the managing
director, obviously
RUTH BROWN, George Brown & Sons

The biggest problem me and George
have would be living up to being him
MICHAEL CLARK, The Old Manor Hotel

Most of the businesses we looked at were started by a father. Around this father figure, in many cases, a certain mythology had arisen – so that whether or not he had done well, the younger generation had a tendency to lionize him. It is interesting to explore why this mythology had grown up. Perhaps the entrepreneurial spirit of the fathers impressed the children; perhaps their often fierce and domineering natures would not brook any disagreement; perhaps they were simply good at blowing their own trumpets. What is clear is that children are easily impressed by their parents. It is also true that everything seems clever when you have no 'inside track'. There was an often-repeated fear that this father figure was going to be a 'hard act to follow'. This exaggeration is a problem, because in accepting it the children are setting themselves up for failure before they even start. It's a lose-lose situation. If you do well it is because your parent handed you something that was already successful; if you do badly it's your own fault.

The AMT Espresso brothers talked about their late father in glowing terms (despite the fact that he had lost the family fortune) and were living out the roles he had allotted them. Apparently he had always insisted that the youngest brother, Alastair, was the engine of the business and that the role of the two others was to support him. This had set the pattern for the state of affairs that subsequently arose – the fact that Alastair was the best negotiator didn't necessarily mean he was the best leader. One of the challenging things about this business was the need to change the relationships between the brothers, to show them that they could all play different roles from those bequeathed to them. In the end, of course, they could not leave the family history behind any more than they could change the status quo and stop arguing. They refused to accept my recommendations for who should take over, and continued to lead the company as before. I noticed that this 'hard act' theme had another deleterious effect on the children: everything needed to be perfect. Sadly, neither life nor business is like that.

The three partners at George Brown & Sons kept referring to 'Pappy', the distant but still powerful grandfather who had set up the business years ago and still had a finger on its pulse. I only met him briefly, but he lived next door to Paul and his influence made it impossible for the three partners to do anything other than try to work together – which was why they were flailing around so badly. The other Alistair, at The Old Manor Hotel in Fife, reminded me of the 'Victorian Dad' comic strip in *Viz*. He was a bully, a workaholic, he rarely praised anyone, and he demanded the same commitment from everyone in the business. His sons, quite capable men in their own right, were very much children in his presence, and certainly jumped when he said 'Jump!' Despite their feeling that his management style was not something they would wish to emulate, he somehow made them feel that they were probably not capable of taking over. What I found fascinating was that even though they had thought through an excellent strategy, they seemed unable to act upon it: something (or, to my mind, someone!) was holding them back.

In a not dissimilar fashion Dudley Moore at County Linen had, as I saw it, effectively been undermining his son Anthony for years, making him feel he would never make it as a manager. Dudley himself hardly came across to me as a strong leader, and his constant, although jovial, presence had so worn his son down that it was no wonder Anthony had little energy for attacking the company's problems. Ironically, the new chairman who emerged to take over from Dudley as mentor and guide had a wonderfully supportive and almost parental approach towards Anthony, which one instinctively felt the younger man needed.

Sir John Starkey was regarded by his family as the most marvellous businessman, but I did not have to dig too deeply to discover that this simply wasn't true. The wedding business was a case in point, bringing in just £12,000 per year despite the fact that every Saturday was booked a year in advance. Norwood Park was in such demand as a venue that I felt the family could increase the profit tenfold simply by putting the prices up. With each business there were startlingly simple measures that I believed would make dramatic improvements in their fortunes. Yet the family myth persisted that Sir John was rarely wrong, and Sir John himself, like other heads of family businesses, was stuck in the belief that his way was usually the right way. Even Robin at Arrow Ford believed he would be a hard act to follow (although in his case other family members did not). It struck me time and again that looking up to a domineering father was a self-fulfilling prophecy. Children who believed in the myth were never going to be able to grow up and operate as independent adults within family businesses.

The Chaplins were an interesting father–son duo, and I never felt that I quite got to the bottom of what was going on at Vernon Road. Richard had bought the fabric-dyeing business and was in charge with his father as chairman, but I suspected that Henry had reservations about his son's management ability. He admitted he had seldom praised Richard, but countered with, 'You haven't done well yet'. Their office layout was a bit of a giveaway. Henry had a huge desk while Richard sat at a small one on the side. Richard recalled noticing as a child that his father was hated by the workers in one factory, so perhaps in a sense he was trying to copy Henry's style. In fact, I believe that Henry was talented and was able to get people to work well for him. I think that without knowing it Richard was trying to prove to his father that he was just as good as, if not better than, him. Maybe this was why he never seemed to feel comfortable in the role of managing director.

● Birth order

Georgie [Henry's wife] is a younger
daughter and you need to be an elder
daughter to be in this sort of situation
LADY STARKEY, Norwood Park

I think there is a pecking order
and I'm a little way down it
RUTH, George Brown & Sons

I am told that there are different characteristics that go with a particular position in a family. Oldest children, for example, are supposed to be ambitious, anxious and perfectionist; middle children are quiet and diplomatic, and feel they never quite match up to the first-born; while youngest children are desperate to be different, often playing the fool or doing something completely unexpected. As the ninth out of ten children myself, I don't really buy this. Yes, I am sure children are raised in slightly different ways as their parents become more experienced and there are more siblings with whom to share or fight, but in my experience everyone has their own particular characteristics, and I have seen many exceptions to these rules. However, I think it is true that siblings in a family slot into different roles – the conformist, the peacemaker, the clown, the brains – and feel some comfort in playing out these roles. What happens when you transfer this group of people into a business context is that the business becomes a vehicle for displaying these entrenched characteristics: people will be treated first and foremost as befits their family 'position' and will find it hard to behave or be seen in a different way. They will often, for example, defer to the oldest child simply because he or she is older. On the positive side, it can mean that there is a nice mix of talents within a family. George and Michael Clark, for example, have complementary skills and were able to use them for the good of the business.

Speaking out of turn

I expect we can all think of times when we have allowed the tiredness and stress from a working day to spill over into our home life, and taken things out on our nearest and dearest. This is usually understandable and sometimes forgivable, and mostly doesn't do much long-term harm. The danger occurs when this happens at work, with people unleashing inappropriate feelings at the wrong time. In a family business there is often no safe outlet to release feelings like these, and they simply explode in a work setting. Then the time and energy expended in damage limitation is enormous. Also, in an effort to avoid a repetition, decisions are deferred or even avoided. In nearly every business we looked at I heard people saying things to one another they would never have said to someone in a normal office environment. When the Starkey family were giving their presentations on how they saw the future of Norwood Park, Suzannah quoted her mother when analysing the motivation of her siblings and their partners: 'Some of us just want to get married here, some of us want to leave here feet first; some of us want an easy life; some of us want to use the house without any responsibilities, and some of us just want to live in a large house.' Strong stuff.

● Intensity

'We're not living above the shop, we're living IN the shop,' commented one family member wryly, and this is a very real problem. It is essential to have a break, and in a family business, on a purely physical level there is often no escape from work. The Gordon-Duff-Penningtons and the Starkeys lived in the 'shop', and had mixed feelings about coming face to face with the customers. 'We feel it is very intrusive, we feel very restricted,' admitted Elizabeth Starkey. The Clarks in Fife all lived in the same house, the sons and their wives with the sons' parents – for workaholic Alistair it was a pleasure to be no more than 105 paces from the hotel. All the older Browns exuded a profound sense of weariness which is typical of people in some family businesses. They worked all the hours God sent without making much difference; they never had a break; and talked endlessly about the business at home. 'Me, Paul and Jim have got to that age where we don't want the hassle,' acknowledged David.

It is essential to have a cut-off between work and home. On an emotional level the intensity engendered by not having one can cause intolerable strain, particularly on married couples. It works both ways: problems in the marriage can affect the business, and problems in the business can wreak havoc on the couple's relationship. It's not good to have a blurring between business and home life, and Peter and Iona were feeling the strain as they attempted to find ways to keep the business afloat, with each of them shooting down the other's new ideas. I felt there was a great deal of antagonism between them, and there was no way they would be able to take the business into the future in a straightforward, clear way, and stand up to the older generation together, unless they started to communicate more effectively. Even their son Euan suspected that I'd advised them to start talking to each other rather than arguing. Finally, on an intellectual level, the closeness between work and family causes problems. It makes it that much harder to stand far enough back from the business to be able to think clearly and plan for the future.

● Generation games

I'm not really into patricide
GEORGE CLARK, The Old Manor Hotel

The terrible thing about parents is that you want to slap them and love them at the same time: it's all very messy and complicated. To a greater or lesser extent we tend to regard our parents with a mixture of irritation and affection. Each generation thinks they can do things better than the one that came before, and children often tend to over-compensate for what they see as failings in their parents: they do everything they can to be different. In a business context this can lead to the management style of successive generations being entirely and deliberately different, and hence to friction. Phyllida, the owner of Muncaster Castle, had a father who raised money by selling off family heirlooms. She was determined not to do this, and developed into a 'hoarder' instead, filling room upon room with clutter. One room was chock-a-block with mattresses; another with dressmakers' dummies! Things were, literally, being left to rot, which made it more difficult for the family to explore the development plans that might save the business. While it can be healthy to come to business management from an entirely new perspective, if you are doing it from a subconscious desire to prove that the older generation had got it wrong, you will be heading for trouble.

● Intimations of mortality

I often feel like his parent, to be
honest. He does irritate me
sometimes, like all children do
SAM, Arrow Ford (about her father)

Part of the problem, too, comes from the children's sense that it is somehow unseemly to be better than their parents at something, or to take over what has been their life's work. They feel a little sad that the older generation is fading away, yet guilty that they are anxious for the baton to be handed over. This deeply contrary emotion was beautifully summed up by George Clark when talking of his father: 'There are times when I have wished I could punch his lights out. I also know that if it got to the point where it was easy to do, I wouldn't want to.' Even after Alistair had handed over more than half his business to his sons, they were still not ready to deprive their father of his position. In the event it was a very emotional handover with entirely understandable sadness at the ending of an era. Lady Starkey, meanwhile, was very anxious about the rush of new ideas coming from her children. 'Who is going to spend the time and money finding the funds, putting the plans in? The jungle is creeping up on us at all times, both inside and out, we've got everything from bugs to deterioration. Who is going to manage this huge growth? We've got to eat, sleep, walk the dog. I am asking the young ones ...'

Family types

We're a very competitive family
ANGUS, AMT Espresso

Unsurprisingly, families tend to have distinctive ways of behaving, where each member will display behaviour that conforms to the way they were brought up. Each will tend to fit in with the emotional surroundings he or she has lived with since birth. In some families, for example, anger is unacceptable, so emotions are buttoned up and people learn to behave in a passive-aggressive manner. In others, they tend not to listen to each other, and are constantly shouting and interrupting. And yet other people are cool and calculating. I suspect this is why family Christmases often get out of hand: too many people behaving in a similar way inevitably results in tension. In a business situation, I leave you to imagine the chaos. Said Angus, 'Our father always pushed us to do better. If I came in with a B he would say, "Son, that's great but it could have been a B plus." If it was an A, "That's brilliant, but it could have been an A plus."' This spirit of competitiveness meant that the brothers were all still trying to outdo each other. They were rarely impressed with what their siblings were doing in the business, and each brother was still chasing the ideal of perfection. At Arrow Ford, Robin Harris and his daughters had not communicated honestly for years, and had become unable to express how they really felt. So Robin kept his troubles to himself, hiding away and feeling unloved. His daughters suffered in silence as they got landed with unfulfilling jobs in a family business that was going nowhere. Yet more than anything they wanted to be able to help their father out, both emotionally and in the business.

● The stagnant gene pool

In a normal business there is a constant influx of new people who bring new ideas, new experiences and new blood. In most family businesses this simply doesn't happen. As a consequence, systems and ways of doing business do not evolve in a natural manner. Stagnation occurs, and the 'We've always done it like this' syndrome takes hold. A skills shortage builds up and, to make matters worse, poor pay and prospects, and the fear of infighting, often lead to bright young family members preferring to go off and get a 'proper job' instead of joining the business they have grown up with – leaving the less able, who either haven't had the will to make it in the outside world or who have simply failed to do so, to fall back on working with dad.

● Family traditions

I like them but I do disagree with them.
It is their bat and ball: it is not a public
company with an MD and a brief to deliver
GINA GOODALL, [non-family] sales director, County Linen

Another handicap that often afflicts family businesses is a nostalgic fondness for continuing with certain business practices and products that have been part of the family for generations. At Norwood Park the fruit farm produced strawberries and apples. While the strawberry side was vastly more profitable, Sir John Starkey had a historical and emotional attachment to the apples that was preventing him from seeing that the future lay on the soft-fruit side. And, of course, there was his preference that his son should be the next head of the business. 'We have always done it this way' is not an acceptable way of carrying on – it leads to the worst kind of amateurish bumbling along. Get with the twenty-first century and start taking the business somewhere.

● Succession

We've all worked jolly hard to get
the business where it is. I don't want
to see it frittered away
ALISTAIR CLARK, The Old Manor Hotel

While all these issues will undoubtedly cause some problems for a family business, they are containable in themselves. The business will probably do OK until it comes to choosing who gets to do what and who gets what – and, in particular, who gets to lead the business. This is when all the complex family stuff conspires to cause terribly muddled thinking and potentially disastrous decision-making. And it was what made the television series such compelling viewing.

'Clogs to clogs in three generations,' observed Robin Harris at Arrow Ford with no trace of irony. It's an old saying, but it has much truth in it. Behind it is the notion that the person who starts the business raises himself up from nothing; he then hands the business to his son, who fritters the money away, leaving nothing for his own children to take on. Succession – who gets to take over as boss – is at the crux of the problems experienced within family businesses. This is where all the thorny issues to do with emotions, history and feuds come to a head. Quite simply, there is not a wide enough choice of candidates for the top job in the first place, and there is rarely an assessment of ability in the process of choosing.

In other businesses a leader will either emerge naturally (particularly if the organization is set up to spot and nurture talent), or if there is no obvious candidate the post may be advertised outside the business to attract potential leaders with a proven track record, sound abilities and relevant experience. Not so in family businesses, oh no. For some reason I am unable to fathom, almost inevitably the heads of these business (even the successful ones) decide to narrow their choice down to the few people who are directly related to them. What an astonishing way to run a business! In some cases they choose the eldest or only son (Henry Starkey), in others they choose the relative nearest in age to themselves (Paul Brown) or the favourite child or the long-lost daughter. Often, unable to choose, they decide to appoint two siblings as joint leaders. A bright 'black sheep' may be overlooked, or – as in the case of Robin Harris's two talented daughters – genuinely capable people are passed over because of a desire not to show favouritism. Their position in the family and how they are related to the owner muddles the perception of their capacity actually to do the job. Even when there is some acknowledgement that a is not up to it, rather than find a more suitable alternative there is a tendency to try to force square pegs into round holes. Sir John Starkey insisted, 'Henry's got to prepare himself to get into the dictator's shoes. He's going to have to go to London Business School.' With strange logic, his solution to the possibility of another of his children ousting Henry from the top job was to stipulate that on their death the estate would not be theirs automatically to pass on as they saw most appropriate. Sir John believed by doing this that he was extending meritocracy, but in my view it may have sounded the death knell for the estate remaining in the family for future generations.

Selecting a new leader from a few close relatives is thought to be preferable to introducing a better but controversial person who may be from the wrong branch of the family, may be a woman, or may not be universally liked. Thus, by taking the line of least resistance, heads of family businesses are opting out of making a well-judged, commercial decision. In rare cases the person selected this way is up to the job; more usually – and fatally – they are not. One very stark lesson from several programmes in the series was: if you want your child to succeed, instil in them the self-confidence that they are capable of doing so.

What this selection process means in reality is that, because normal judgement is suspended, the wrong person is chosen for all the wrong reasons. That person is then saddled with a job they feel honour- and duty-bound to take on; but it is a job they are fundamentally not cut out for. Tim and Anthony Moore were a prime example of this. Terrified of allowing County Linen to fall apart 'on their watch', they were doomed at best to unsatisfying lives, and at worst to humiliating failure. And even Peter, married to the highly competent heiress Iona Duff-Pennington, commented: 'There's a crushing sense of duty that keeps you working every hour that God gives.'

Are family issues getting in the way?

*Things have come out of your
mouth that were in my head*
ROBIN HARRIS, Arrow Ford

*I kind of expected what you
were going to say anyway*
HENRY STARKEY, Norwood Park

Yes, they are. You don't need Gerry Robinson to arrive with a film crew to tell you that in all family businesses the family issues play back into the business in a highly destructive way. I don't believe I told anyone anything that they did not already know at some level – but had chosen not to recognize. To bring it down to specifics, though, look very carefully at the way meetings, decision-making, communication and leadership are handled. Stand back as much as you can and try hard to be clear-headed and observant.

Are your meetings too frequent or very long? ☐
Are your meetings too short, or non-existent? ☐
Are there issues that are taking up business time that have nothing
to do with the business itself? ☐
Is there a sense of confusion about where the business is going? ☐
Are there people who refuse to speak to each other? ☐
Are there frequent arguments? ☐
Are decisions being made quickly and sensibly? ☐
Are there decisions which, having been made, are not acted upon? ☐
Are there things that ought to be happening, but are not? ☐
Are there some people in the business who operate separately, making
their own decisions, relying on their own mysterious expertise
which is rarely questioned by others? ☐
Have most people only ever worked for the business itself? ☐
Is there singularity of leadership? ☐
Do you know who you report to and who reports to you? ☐
Do people know where they fit in? ☐

You don't need to add up your scores this time. If you have taken on board the lessons of this book you will know exactly how bad your problems are, and this list is merely to focus your mind on them.

What to do about all this

At the end of the day it's for the good
of the firm, isn't it, and that's
what we're talking about
JIM, George Brown & Sons

My sister has a very successful cleaning and security business that she set up from scratch twenty years ago. Its staff includes her daughter and two sons, and part of her success has been in playing to their strengths and putting them into roles that suit them perfectly. The daughter is good at people management, so she deals with the staff. One of the sons is likeable and charming, and therefore great in sales. The other son is the hard-nosed business brain of the family, so he now runs the company. I expect they have their arguments, but it is a very nice, close family and there is no fundamental antagonism. This separation of roles, and consensus about who was to lead the company, happened without the world falling apart, and my sister has now handed the business over to the three of them. It will be interesting to watch what happens when the next generation of children comes through. Of course there is no compelling reason for them to go into the family business at all.

Finding solutions to the problems that the companies in *I'll Show Them Who's Boss* were going through was relatively easy: I had usually decided within a few days what my recommendations were to be. What was much more of a struggle was getting the families to accept my suggestions – for all the complex reasons described above. It was an emotionally draining experience for me, and I am aware that I caused a good deal of upset in many cases. I often found myself telling people what they did not want to hear, but to be honest there was no point in going through the exercise if I couldn't be frank and open about my recommendations. I do believe the businesses came out of the hell I put them through in better shape to face the future. It has got to be better to receive a timely kick up the backside than to do nothing and slide into failure. Of course, if you are running a family business it is very hard to identify problems and solutions without an objective observer, but it is not impossible. All businesses can be demystified by looking at relationships between people, and getting the right people in the right place. The fact that some of the people happen to be related shouldn't be the kiss of death if it is handled sensitively and pragmatically. It goes without saying that I think you should follow the management advice in the rest of this book – but if you are determined to lessen the negative impact your family may be having on your business, there are some other steps you can take. All these suggestions are based on the fundamental principle of *separating the family issues from the business concerns.*

● Go out as a family

*I think if we could now and then support
each other instead of trying so hard to
outdo each other and prove how smart
we are, we'd get a lot further*
Angus, AMT Espresso

When any family gets together you can expect a rowdy, healthy banter with certain stories always getting an airing, various people ribbed and teased, the shared history discussed, silly jokes exchanged. We love talking about what happened when we were children, what our parents and grandparents were like, and how our children are doing. This is really important, but this closeness can often be missing in a family business because the daily round of more pressing commercial issues gets in the way. Take the time to enjoy being with each other. If you have had an argument with someone, remember that underneath it all you really care for each other. Try to recall what it is about the other person that is special, good and positive. Do everything in your power to re-establish friendly family relations – it would be incredibly sad to sacrifice the enormous strength that can be drawn from a loving, supportive family just for the sake of running a business together.

● Create a 'family issues' forum

The idea behind this is to have a more formal opportunity to separate the negative emotional and family 'stuff' that is going on from the business side of the organization. Have a regular, non-business, social gathering of the senior family group in which any problems can be expressed and talked through openly and rationally. This is not going to be easy to do at first, but with drinks and a few nibbles barriers will be broken down and after a few sessions people will get the idea. Introduce the first gathering by explaining how family issues can get in the way of the smooth running of the business, and that what you are hoping to achieve by having a separate forum, perhaps once a month, is to get them dealt with before they build up and cause problems. If people understand that they must try to reserve their niggles and gripes and grudges for this special meeting you may start to go some way to clarifying the business environment, and they should become less frustrated. Be humorous, discuss things that have been going right as well as wrong, and don't take yourselves too seriously.

● Establish a formal grievance procedure

All organizations should have a system whereby staff can safely record a complaint or a problem they are experiencing with another member of staff. People should know exactly what the process is, who deals with the problem in the first instance, what happens next, and how arbitration works. This will ease tensions enormously, and it may be a good idea for this to feed into the issues forum.

● Be frank about business pressures

The other side of this coin is that some families never get together to discuss business issues, which can happen if the managing director is reluctant to worry family members. When a business has reached an impasse, or if there are serious financial concerns, it can be refreshing and rewarding to widen the discussion of where to go and what to do. In a sense this is what I was doing by asking family members for presentations on where they saw the future of the businesses, and by having quiet one-to-one discussions. In many cases there emerged – along with considerable friction – a wealth of ideas, often well thought through, for taking the businesses forward in imaginative and practical ways. In one instance it was the first time the family had ever sat down together to discuss business. It can be very hard indeed to balance the commercial reality on the one hand with who is going to run the company on the other – and this was at the heart of the television series. But a month or so of real, hard debate and a bit of conflict is not a huge price to pay for getting things right in the long run.

● Recognize people for what they can do, not who they are

Separate the feelings you have for someone from a reasonable analysis of their strengths and weaknesses. If you are considering promoting them, play to their abilities – don't try to change them to suit the job you would like them to do. This is difficult, and there are conflicting impulses at work here. As a parent you want to treat all your children equally; as head of a family company you feel you need to select a leader from among them; and as a business person you need to sort out what each one is most suited to doing. Be tough, and be objective: as a parent you do actually know what each child excels at, and what each will be happy doing. Curb your ambitions for them – the cruellest thing you can do to children is force them into something they are simply not cut out to do. This will only set them up for a long string of failures and insecurities. It is more courageous, and kinder in the end, to make another decision. After all, business is not really that important. What is important is people's lives and happiness – and surely at heart what parents want for their children is a decent life. In fact everyone is always happier when the difficult decision has been made. The world doesn't fall apart – people move on.

If the opposite is the case, and you have not been promoting a certain person for whatever reason, stop and identify their talents – it is crucial to recognize and cultivate good people coming up through the family, and also to spot good non-family members and take a risk with them. Don't let them feel a layer of family permafrost is preventing them from rising up through the ranks, as happened with the ousted Gordon Dick at County Linen. Make a supreme effort to be objective and realistic. If you are unsure about someone, try talking to people who report to the individual to help establish exactly what they are good at, and if there are areas in which they could improve. It is better to go behind someone's back to acquire information of this kind than to risk the long-term damage to a business of making the wrong decision. Keep probing, keep asking, and question all your assumptions. 'The what and the who' is at the heart of what you should be examining.

● Be your own person

If you are a member of the younger generation and are in line for leadership of the business, do not take it on just because it is your turn. Make your own choices, follow your own wishes and career path. Be prepared to jump ship, but don't look upon it as running away; rather as opening up opportunities for someone else who may be genuinely excited about the business. If you do take the job, don't try to copy exactly what has gone before no matter how much you respect and love the previous leader.

● Make commercial decisions, not family decisions

All the big decisions you make in a company have an emotional impact. In a family business these emotions are writ larger. It is vital to ensure that your decision is made on sound commercial grounds first, and deal with the people issues later. If you need to close a factory, axe a product, open a new office, or acquire a competitor, see it as a purely business decision. Do not let any ideas of 'family tradition' prevent you from doing what is right. If you mess up the business you will do a great deal of harm to everyone. Be hard in making your decision, but be as kind as you can in executing it.

● Do not underpay

Although I believe that money is not the great motivator it is cracked up to be, you cannot expect people to accept low pay and poor working conditions simply because they are related to you. If you do, you will lose the talented people that you should be falling over yourself to keep.

● Get some outside perspective

Before you bring family members into the business, ensure that they have worked elsewhere first. This will bring in new ideas and experience even if it doesn't bring in new blood. You may have waited years to get your hands on them, but patience is a virtue here. Let them develop some independence – and perhaps even check out the competition!

● In matters of succession, bring in an independent adviser

No matter how hard you try, you cannot really be objective when promoting your own and, as was abundantly clear in the television programmes, the choice of who is to lead a business is the single thing that determines whether or not it will be successful. It is imperative to find an objective person who will keep emotions out of the process, so choose a friend of a friend to come in and be part of some sort of selection procedure. This should be a person whose judgement you trust, and who is seen by the people in your company to be sensible, experienced and trustworthy. Do not choose an old friend, and avoid anyone who might have a personal axe to grind or who might be tempted to agree with what you think you would like to do. Even if you are sure of your choice (especially if you are sure), be hard-nosed, be intellectually honest, and be prepared to listen to what the adviser says. Rupert Murdoch, take note!

● Separate ownership from management

Problems arise when owners without the necessary talent think they have to be managers. Remember that a business can be owned by family members without their actually having to run it. Conversely, if managers end up with the opportunity to own a company by buying out the owners that can provide an enormous boost to morale and productivity, and give the business new clarity and a new lease of life. Ownership as an adjunct to managerial talent is fantastic.

And finally (if I haven't made myself clear by now) ...

Keep the family out of it!

It is often said that the skills of good parenting are similar to the skills of good management. Being clear in what you are asking, setting boundaries, being consistent in what you are saying and how you are saying it, and offering a firm but caring guiding hand – all these are aspects of both parenting and management. Yet the fact that the two are similar in this way does not mean that you should combine parenting and management in one glorious family entity.

The family is a great vehicle for starting a business, but it is a lousy vehicle for continuing it, and this is where things will go wrong. For goodness' sake stop trying to keep the business within the family – there is no inherent commercial value in doing so. Why do people continue in this clannish, dynastic behaviour? It is baffling. Your starting-point should be to ensure that your children aren't involved: get the business up and running, then bring in a leader from outside. You don't have to be there, and it won't fall apart if your son isn't the boss – in fact, it is more likely to fall apart if he is. So don't groom your children for the business; don't send them off specifically to gain relevant experience elsewhere. Let them do what they want to do. Fight like hell against bringing them into the business, and have family members in it only if they genuinely, passionately and desperately want to work there after working elsewhere. Then you will have the best of all worlds.

CHAPTER EIGHT

▶ Management myths

Most management advice is rubbish. Throw the rule books out of the window, and concentrate on getting about three or four things right

I don't know if it's got something to do with the contrariness of the Irish, or whether it is because I come from a large, working-class family, but I have never been happy with accepting the traditional way of doing things. During the course of my career I have run some fairly big organizations, and I think by now I have a pretty clear view of how companies function, what can go wrong, and how to make them work better. Although I sometimes feel like an alien being who has landed on a different planet, I think it is really important to challenge the status quo and always be clear, open and direct. This has inevitably got me into well-publicized trouble with members of the Establishment, particularly those who have disagreed with my approach or left companies after my arrival. Funnily enough, I don't see myself as ruthless, lazy or irresponsible; more a breath of fresh air. Running a business really isn't that complicated, although people tend to behave as if is. There are a few simple things you must get absolutely right, and this book has been about these few things. One strong leader who has the qualities of clarity, consistency and passion, together with excellent people who can follow through on detail – these are the ingredients for success. Making *I'll Show Them Who's Boss* was a wonderful opportunity for me to show how by getting these few things right you really can make dramatic and long-lasting improvements to a business of any size.

I said at the beginning of this book that if you only read one chapter it should be this one. In many ways it sums up what I have discussed in much greater detail in the rest of the book, and I make no apologies for repeating some of the points I have already made. While I would be the first to admit that there are no 'quick fixes' in business, and any changes should be sensitively and thoughtfully handled, it can help to stand back from the way you might have been doing things by examining what I see as the twenty-seven 'myths' that damage businesses. So here they are, in no particular order.

Myth 1:

You need to be cool and detached to be a good business person

I think this is to do with a kind of British reserve, the idea that to be successful in business you keep your distance, analyse the market and make some clever financial decisions. Wrong. I have seen people intellectualize a business to death. Business is all about people, and all about emotions, and the best leaders I know have fantastic people skills. To get to the nub of what is going on in a business, talk to the staff. There are a number of things that destroy companies, and one of them is low morale. To improve business performance, get the right people in the right jobs, make them feel that they're really up for what they're doing, and that the business is fundamentally OK, and your problems are virtually solved.

Myth 2:

The longer you work, the more you contribute

This strikes me as just about the saddest thing about business life. At any level of management, if you are working all the hours God sends, you will be causing more harm than good. When I was chief executive of the leisure group Granada I got some flak from some sections of the press for stating that if I couldn't fit my job into a nine-to-five day I was either being unreasonable or I was mucking it up. But I stand by this, and in fact quite a few people thanked me for taking a stand against the unreasonable hours that are often expected. Maxwell Joseph, who set up Grand Met and turned it into a multimillion-pound industry, worked only three days a week. He was very clear about the big issues, he had good people working for him, and he followed up steadily but not on a daily basis.

At the most senior level, working long hours is dangerous for the business for several reasons:

- You start to invent things to fill the time. You come up with half-thought-through ideas, you half suggest them to your staff, and they run off to investigate them. This is going to be stressful, wasteful and frustrating. Be very careful before you set unnecessary things in motion.
- If you are working long hours you establish an unhealthy culture whereby everyone who works for you feels they have to sit at their desks late into the night as well.
- You very easily lose the 'big picture stuff' because you inevitably get mired in small details.
- You fail to delegate, thereby making everyone's job less interesting.
- You are in danger of meddling with other people's domains. Remember that they will often know more than you do, and know different things. Let them get on with their jobs.
- You become tired, and tiredness is a killer of clear thinking. There is no way you can approach your job with enthusiasm if you are working twelve hours a day.
- Ultimately you risk becoming stressed, depressed and burnt out.

If you discipline yourself to get some perspective, concentrate on the few big things and learn to delegate effectively, you will find that lots of the small stuff that you have been panicking about will melt away, and that problems you might have sweated over are actually better sorted out by someone else. You are not indispensable.

Myth 3:

You need to be a financial genius to run a company

Numbers are not magical. They are no more than a record of what the business has done, or projections of what someone thinks the business might do. One of the keenest fears felt by business leaders is that they will be exposed for the terrible weakness of not being able to understand the accounts. And many people at all levels believe they are at a huge disadvantage if they are not from a financial background or good with numbers. As long as you are business literate and can pick up the basics you will be fine. I once came across someone who ran a very successful parcel-delivery company in the Midlands called Bees Transport. He didn't have a clue about the numbers, but his ability with logistics and skills with people enabled him to run a very tight business indeed. He simply had an intuitive feel for things that were going wrong.

You do, of course, need someone to take care of the finances, and this person needs to be willing and able to explain the basics to you and others. Many accountants are in love with the process, and they revel in the fact that you can't understand it. What is worse, most financial information is badly presented and contributes nothing towards the success of a business.

- If you don't understand, keep on asking until you do.
- Don't be afraid to show your ignorance – it is often endearing. If you are really trying and still don't understand something, I'd bet the person explaining it to you doesn't understand it either.
- If your accountant can't produce reports that you understand easily and can use, give him a couple more chances to do so, then get someone in who can do what you want.
- Read and inwardly digest the following:

In profit and loss terms there are only three things that affect the bottom line:

1 Price
Find out what customers will pay. (I find they often feel better if they're paying more!) It goes without saying that the product or service you are supplying needs to be excellent.

2 Volume
Sell, sell, sell. Good marketing and a first-class sales team are crucial.

3 Costs

Be vigilant. Do you really need to spend it? Does it really contribute to the business? Keep questioning.

Myth 4:

You need a business background to run a company

If this were really true no one would ever try anything new. To run a company you need guts, clarity, nous, vision and passion – and above all, a capacity to get on with people. More important than specific business knowledge is an ability to select the best staff, to know what makes them tick, and to make them feel good about working for you and enthusiastic about carrying out their jobs. It obviously helps to know something about how a business is run – I have seen people from academia, for example, really struggle – so you should be in no doubt about the importance of marketing, good systems, and a lot of selling.

The higher up an organization you are, the less you need to know about the detailed running of the business. Making a brilliant television programme is very different from managing a television company, and you can buy detailed skills and knowledge. Whatever you do, don't pretend to know about something you don't. If you have joined an industry you are not familiar with, you should be able to pick up the key issues within a few weeks at most, and you must know whom to ask if you need to find out specifics. There is a huge benefit, in fact, to coming in from a fresh angle. The very fact that you don't know much gives you the ability to question why things are done in a particular way. Turn your lack of knowledge to your advantage.

Myth 5:

It is really difficult and quite frightening to raise money for business expansion

It is a common misconception that 'the City' is a scary place, but we forget that there are hundreds of institutions whose role in life is to find good companies and able people in which to invest. Indeed, they need you more than you need them. Fear of approaching large banking institutions can so often stop companies developing. It is not hard to get backing for good businesses. I also don't subscribe to the myth that bankers are short-term thinkers. I suspect it is often underperforming companies who complain that they're not well understood in the City.

There are a few simple things to bear in mind:

- Work out how much money you need, and triple it. Costs are always much higher than you estimate, particularly building works, and things take longer to happen.
- If you need a lot of money and don't know how to go about it, start with your current bank. They will be keen to help, and they may even have their own venture capital or broking arm.
- Aim to investigate three or four sources of funding (you will find a huge choice on the internet just by looking up Venture Capital through one of the search engines). Narrow the sources down to one when you are confident of getting a deal with people you trust.
- The lender must have confidence in you as the leader of the project. Be very well informed, be enthusiastic, and be able to answer questions.
- Lenders will tend to throw money at you far too easily, so be selective. Be clear about the terms of the deal, and how much it is going to cost you. A good rapport with the person who is organizing your funding is essential, so choose the one with whom you get on best.
- It is in the leader's interest for your business to be successful, and you will be amazed at how quickly you will get good advice from them.

Myth 6:

You need to make every decision yourself

You will do more harm by trying to run everything than by standing back. Poor managers always try to get involved at too detailed a level; they want to run everything; they think they know everything. I don't know whether this comes from insecurity, or whether it is some kind of power trip, but beware of feeling that only you can do it. There is a real discipline in being able to set your own criteria and then stand back. You must develop antennae to pick up signs from people when they feel you are getting too involved.

What can often happen is that people who are frightened of decision-making will come to you for advice, hoping that you will take on the responsibility. The best way to deal with this is to bat the problem back by saying, 'I don't know as much about this as you do, I'm not sure about it, but I'm prepared to be convinced. If YOU think it is a good idea then do a bit more work on it and give it a go.' You will find most problems miraculously go away, and if they don't, you can be sure that the person concerned is absolutely committed to making whatever it is work. It is a superb system for filtering out those exciting but silly ideas that pop up, for encouraging development of real judgement, and for giving people autonomy. It is also important for decisions to be made at the relevant level. For example, someone on the bought ledger side who is used to writing out small cheques will have a much better sense of what is value for money than someone higher up in the organization. After delegating, make sure you know what you have asked of whom: follow-up is crucial or things will unravel.

Myth 7:
You need to have lots of ideas to be a leader

Quite the opposite is true: it helps to be the person with a bucket of cold water. The head of an organization who has too many ideas is actually a pain in the backside. Nothing will be followed through effectively and the organization's energy will be diffused. It is not your job to be 'creative' in this way. There are plenty of other things for a leader to be doing. (See the rest of this book!) What you do need is a clear vision. We think of someone like Bill Gates as a person who has ideas all the time; in fact he had one big idea, which was to retain the rights for his software and lease them out, rather than make a lot of money early on by selling them. Ernie Harrison, originally an accountant with the defence instrument company Racal, was so convinced that mobile phones were the future that he pulled out all the stops to get the government franchise and focused all his energies on Vodafone, then got it going and motivated people to work really hard for him. Twenty years later it is one of the biggest companies in the world.

So let the ideas people have the ideas. Your job is to make sure that everybody else is getting on and implementing the good ones. A word of warning about ideas people: never let them manage anything. I know it sounds unfair, but 'creatives' are better kept in a position where they can continue to create.

Myth 8:

The strategic plan is a thing of beauty and a joy for ever

I have seen more time wasted on strategic plans than on anything else in business. In my experience they tend to be wonderfully produced tomes that never see the light of day after their first presentation. Hands up whoever has a SWOT chart hidden away in a filing cabinet. Throw it away! Have you got a strategy department? Close it down. As the leader of the business you are responsible for strategy. It is your key role. Strategy should be a statement of what you want to achieve over the next five years, and the things that you need to do to get there. It should be realistic, but stretching. It should be measurable along the way, with dates. And it should specify exactly who is going to do what. You should alos allow for spontaneity – often strategy documents can limit a leader's thinking. Sometimes you need to be able to respond quickly to a change in market conditions, a new business opportunity, or a product that suddenly takes off. Run with it, and ask questions later.

From your strategic plan you then drill down to your short-term plan for the first year. THEN DO IT. Delegate tasks, and follow up rigorously.

Myth 9:

It's a grey area

There are no grey areas in business, but it is something we use as an excuse for not facing up to tough issues. People I met through *I'll Show Them Who's*

Boss were specialists in grey areas. The muddle is not intrinsically in the business, it's in your head. Be suspicious of things that you don't understand, and even more suspicious if someone explains them to you and you still don't understand. Accepting a lack of clarity is mostly a way of avoiding difficult issues, which more often than not will be people issues. You know someone isn't up to the job, but you let them carry on. Someone can't explain the reasons behind a fall in their figures, and you let them get away with it. You are aware that things are being done in a less than optimum way, but you don't face up to changing this. You have an overstock of certain products, but you accept this as just one of those things.

If there is something you are unhappy or unclear about, keep coming back to it: probe, ask questions, be intellectually honest. Split the issues into clear areas, tackle the biggest and the others will fall into place. The person I've most admired for this was Alex Bernstein at Granada, who had a fantastic ability to think things through properly, arrive at a conclusion, and accept that conclusion even if he did not personally like it. There is a rigorous discipline about really thinking things through that conflicts with our human desire to shrink from uncomfortable truths. I think there is something in us, too, that is comfortable with a fudge, happy to muddle along. There's a great line from 'Diamonds and Rust' by Joan Baez, where she expresses her unwillingness to recall the pain of losing Bob Dylan's love: 'I need some of that vagueness now/It's all come back too clearly.'

Myth 10:
The board will decide

Wrong, wrong, wrong. It is not the role of the board to run the business. The board is there to be the last stop, and to prevent daft things happening. The board is a committee, and committees can't 'run' anything. It is lethal to let them near any decision, even though you may often find that they want to be involved. If boards are having to vote on issues, then you have a major problem. Decision-making is the job of the leader and his team, so the day I find myself making the key decisions at Allied Domecq is the day I know I have the wrong chief executive.

The real job of the board is:

1 To make sure they have the right chief executive.
2 To give advice on major moves that the company wants to make, and to have the final veto.
3 To ensure that the company is behaving legally and in accordance with accepted business codes.

It is the job of the management team to run the company and ensure that the board is happy with what it is doing. Unless decisions are taken at the operating level, things go badly.

Myth 11:

You create good teams by knowing about personality types

I'm sorry, but I find personality archetypes as formulated by so-called experts such as Meredith Belbin and the Myers-Briggs group about as useful a guide to people's performance and potential as their star signs. You will no doubt have come across these fascinating personality profile questionnaires on training courses. So what if you are supposedly a certain 'type'? What good is it going to do you? We know everyone is different. When selecting people for your team, the most important thing is to look for ones who are decent, honest, bright and capable. You will find that good people will naturally work together as a team, will interrelate well and will want each other to succeed. And while I'm on the subject of teams, don't send people off on those terrible outward-bound weekends. Have a party instead.

Myth 12:

I want it done my way

Very dangerous! So many people fall into the trap of believing that there is only one way of doing things. Leaders fall in love with the sound of their own voice, they regard their role as being to pontificate and pronounce on every issue and become autocrats or, worse, little dictators. Without realizing it, they create a climate of fear in which resentments easily grow. Don't take this path. Establish what results you want and then allow those responsible to achieve them in their own way. Set end results, not methods. If you specify exactly how something should be done, you leave no space for someone's own inventiveness, intuition and personal development. Give them the outline and let them colour it in.

Myth 13:
I don't like him so I can't work with him

I call this the 'happy family' myth. It is the belief that you have to like all of those who work for you or with you, and it is nonsense. I know many people I wouldn't want to spend my days with, but who are excellent at their jobs. Make a distinction in your mind between their sociability and their capacity to carry out their job. Office life should be enjoyable, but it doesn't have to be a bundle of laughs all the time. If someone is capable, intelligent and a good worker, be big enough to recognize their contribution and leave them alone. Trust and respect are enough in themselves. Be aware of your own flashpoints: I can't bear cold people, and I can't bear arrogance, but I know at least one pompous and overbearing chief executive who also happens to be very smart. If you have a very bad feeling about someone it may be an indication of an underlying problem, but do be careful. I have seen so many instances of people of real talent being tossed aside simply because they don't get on with the boss.

Myth 14:
Consultants will give you the best management advice

There is a fatal flaw at the heart of the consultancy industry. When you bring in a team of consultants to make recommendations for turning your business around two things happen. Firstly they talk to everyone concerned and play back to you what you already know. This in itself is fine, as you probably have not organized your thoughts in a systematic way and it can be helpful to have the issues laid out clearly. Secondly they will make a series of recommendations. The flaw is that because you are paying them for their advice they will not give you their full and honest view, which could often really be to say that you as leader are not good enough. Their recommendations will stop short of saying the unsayable. As I have said countless times, if you have the right person at the top of an organization everything else will fall into place. The fact that you have called in the consultants is in my view a warning sign that your leadership is faulty. Because I was not being paid by any of the businesses in the *I'll Show Them Who's Boss* series, I could tell people this without fear of losing a consultancy contract. In the past, whenever I have looked at a business with a view to acquiring it I have always been interested to see if they have spent money on consultants. This is a clear sign of a weakness in top management and an acknowledgement that they need to be sorted out.

Myth 15:
Everyone can be a leader

Oh dear, no. This is a very unfortunate and wrong-headed trend in management thinking. And it is a contradiction in terms. People are what they are, they have innate characteristics, and it is impossible to rebuild them as something entirely different. I hate the idea that everyone can be homogenized into happy shiny leaders – it is a cruel and artificial promise, although I can see why certain industries have grown up to promote the idea. (Just browse through the self-help section of your local bookshop!) If you try to force people into something they cannot do, they will fail. If you try to force yourself into a new role because you feel you ought to, you will be unhappy. Leadership is something you can either do or you can't. Having said that, if you are genuinely interested in it and already have some of the basic characteristics, there are definitely certain skills you can learn. But come on, we need variety – everyone wanting to do the same job would be disastrous.

Myth 16:

To be a boss you have to be bossy

The exact opposite is true, but there is a definite confusion here – perhaps because the words are similar. Bossiness is very close to bullying. It is an angry, arrogant, hectoring way of behaving that treats people as inferior, makes them feel small, and takes no account of them as individuals. I see it as a terrible sign of insecurity and panic. Not only should you not try to be bossy, there is also no need to be loud and extrovert. In the *I'll Show Them Who's Boss* series, many of the leaders who were failing threw their weight around in this way. As a contrast, the new leaders who came through were typified by their great people skills, and their ability to motivate people to perform without having to resort to playground tactics. You have to have the staff with you, and you cannot do this by dragooning them. If you think of people you have worked for whom you have liked and respected, I think you'll find that the fact you were happy to do things for them had nothing to do with their forcing you, and a lot to do with their effortless authority and genuine motivational skills, and the sense that you were dealing with a decent human being.

Myth 17:

If you're not the boss you can't do anything positive for the company

This is a cop-out. There are very real ways in which you can have a hugely positive effect on the business and, indeed, your boss needs talented people to come up through the ranks. I have known plenty of companies in which the person who was behind change and innovation was not actually the one in control. No matter how lowly you think you are, start with the person you report to. Don't whinge about problems; be positive, and offer solutions that you have thought through properly. You will find that people are generally up for trying something if it is well presented.

The way to ensure that you have your say even if you're not the top banana is to:

- table items for meetings
- push, push and push (but nicely) for your ideas to be taken seriously
- back up your ideas with solid research
- be enthusiastic but realistic
- start small: prove that minor changes work and you'll be able to build up to the biggies

Myth 18:

Corporate governance is a real business necessity

I hate with a passion the current obsession with increased corporate governance. The ever-heavier burden of regulations that govern how you run your company have taken more and more management time that could have been used for creativity and innovation. How absurd is this idea that things can be perfectly governed and controlled and secured. Reality is just not like this: there are some things you simply cannot legislate for. What is going on? Our personal freedom is being eroded everywhere we look. In a business context, as a shareholder, your only real protection is the honesty and decency of those who run the company. I believe the people who run a business should be allowed to get on with it: no amount of corporate governance will stop the next Enron; nor will it stop a powerful tycoon from behaving dishonestly if that is what he wants to do. After all, it is easy to tick the boxes, to have the committee, to have codes of practice in place, to give your directors a list of their rules and responsibilities. What a handy cover! If we've ticked the boxes it must be all right – maybe we don't need to think about it any further.

Myth 19:

If you look after the pennies, the pounds will look after themselves

We all grew up with this, didn't we? It might be true if you're a kid with 50p pocket-money, but it is just not true in a business. In my experience, a daft emphasis on small savings blinds people to the big picture. If you penny-pinch it is a sure sign that you are mucking it up. You can't worry about that kind of minutiae and also focus on the key issues facing your business. Leave the detail to others. Your job is to keep a firm hand on the tiller and steer the organization towards its goals without being deflected by small stuff and overwhelmed by the daily details that hit your desk. In my view, when you are busy looking after the pennies, someone else runs away with the pounds.

Myth 20:

The management of change is every leader's nightmare

It doesn't have to be. Just because people are terrified of change, it doesn't mean that therefore you should fear the process of managing it. The world is changing at a scary rate, but we have to produce periods of finite stability within which we can operate. Create a microclimate in which change is acceptable, and make it appear stable. We need security, and we need a leader we can trust to make us feel OK about what is happening in our world. Bring in the changes quickly, understand how people will feel, and establish a new secure reality as soon as possible. If you need to make redundancies, do it properly and do it once, then concentrate on reassuring and enthusing those who remain. If you cannot do this, your business will soon become obsolete.

Myth 21:

Money is a great motivator

I don't believe that it is really money that gets people out of bed in the mornings. Obviously they need to earn a fair salary, and talented people should be rewarded, but there are more important elements that influence them. A sense that they are doing well, are being appreciated, have good working conditions, a friendly atmosphere, and a knowledge that the business they work for is doing well are all crucial. A senior management bonus system will destabilize a business, cause arguments and prompt resignations. If you have one, get rid of it.

Myth 22:
Put it in writing

This is one of the greatest obstacles to good communication I can think of. There is far too much written stuff whizzing around offices, and 90 per cent of it is worthless. Of course you need contracts in writing, and you need brief written *aides-mémoire*. But most of what people write is to do with justifying themselves, blowing their own trumpets, covering their backs, or getting out of decision-making. If staff receive too many e-mails and reports and memos, they will start to ignore them. By far the best approach is to speak to people directly – this saves time, avoids misunderstandings and is much nicer. And if you cannot do that, pick up the phone.

Myth 23:
A meeting will sort it out

Wrong. A meeting will probably make it worse, raising more questions than it solves. Most organizations have far too many meetings. People love a get-together, a chat and a chance to find out what their colleagues are up to – but meetings are not the place for this. Look very carefully at how many you have and try to cut the number in half. Know what their purpose is, keep them short and to the point.

Myth 24:
It is beyond our control

Really? This is what business leaders say when they are overtaken by events. When profits fall drastically they are unwilling to blame themselves, so they blame interest rates, 9/11, a hot summer, or a change in technology. I am not suggesting that these things can necessarily be foreseen, but I am suggesting that all businesses should be aware of where they are most vulnerable and plan accordingly. Watch your competitors, look for warning signs of a downturn, know where you are exposed, and know which products and markets are high risk for you. Tight control and heightened awareness is your only insurance against the unexpected.

Myth 25:
It's not as bad as all that

I have never in my life been pleasantly surprised by things being less bad than people have portrayed. There is a kind of naïve optimism that things will turn out OK if you just work a bit harder, pay someone a little more, move into a new office, launch a new product. Wrong. Short-term problems are more often than not long-term bad news, and unless you fact up to them quickly and sort them out they will spell the demise of the business (see Myth 26).

Myth 26:
If it ain't broke, don't fix it

This makes some sense, when it simply means 'Don't meddle', However, I am sure it is used as an excuse for failing to act. Indeed, it could be the story of the British motor-car or motor-cycle industry. I believe it would be better to say 'When it is working and there is no panic, let's use the time to see how we can do it better'. Innovation is inseparable from progress.

Myth 27:
It can't be done

Yes it can! I have often come across this attitude. People in an organization know the business is in trouble and that something drastic needs to happen, but the obstacles are seemingly insurmountable. In fact it can be done, as I have seen time and again. What a company needs at this stage is new management – a new leader with a dynamic new vision. As far as money is concerned, most banks will see you through a tough time if you can point to assets and a strong plan for the future. Through strength and enterprise, and the ability to get things done, problems start to melt away and there is a genuine improvement. Everything starts at the top and filters down. Within an amazingly short space of time there is a dramatic shift in morale, and this in turn assists with the turnaround of the business. You only need to watch *I'll Show Them Who's Boss* to see how this works in practice.

Good luck!